Tim Bowden is an acclaimed oral historian, broadcaster, and radio and television documentary maker who for many years, as host of *Backchat*, was known as the voice of the ABC. He is the author of six books including *The Silence Calling: Australians in Antarctica*, *Antarctica and Back in Sixty Days* and *One Crowded Hour: Neil Davis, Combat Cameraman*.

penelope goes west

On the road from Sydney to Margaret River and back

TIM BOWDEN

ALLEN & UNWIN

This edition published in 2000
First published in 1999

Allen & Unwin
9 Atchison Street, St Leonards NSW 2065 Australia
Phone: (61 2) 8425 0100
Fax: (61 2) 9906 2218
E-mail: frontdesk@allen-unwin.com.au
Web: http://www.allen-unwin.com.au

National Library of Australia
Cataloguing-in-Publication entry:

Bowden, Tim, 1937–
Penelope goes west : on the road from Sydney to Margaret River and back.

Bibliography.
ISBN 1 86508 307 0.

1. Eyre, Edward John, 1815-1901. 2. Bowden, Tim, 1937– Journeys. 3. Australia - Discovery and exploration. I. Title.

919.4

Set in 12/15pt Caslon 540 by Midland Typesetters
Printed and bound by McPherson's Printing Group, Maryborough, Vic.
10 9 8 7 6 5 4 3 2 1

contents

ACKNOWLEDGMENTS vii
INTRODUCTION x
MAP xv

1 **Penelope and The Manor** 1

2 **Explorers and Prehistoric Ants** 19

3 **We Join the Grey Nomads** 49

4 **When Can I Buy Another Tomato?** 75

5 **Cocktails at Six** 98

6 **Lucky Bay, Wind Farms and Space Junk** 122

7 **A Fiery Christmas** 147

8 **Rolls-Royce Chardonnay at a BMW Price** 175

9 **A Whale of a Time** 208

10 **The Last Bush Camp** 231

BIBLIOGRAPHY 241

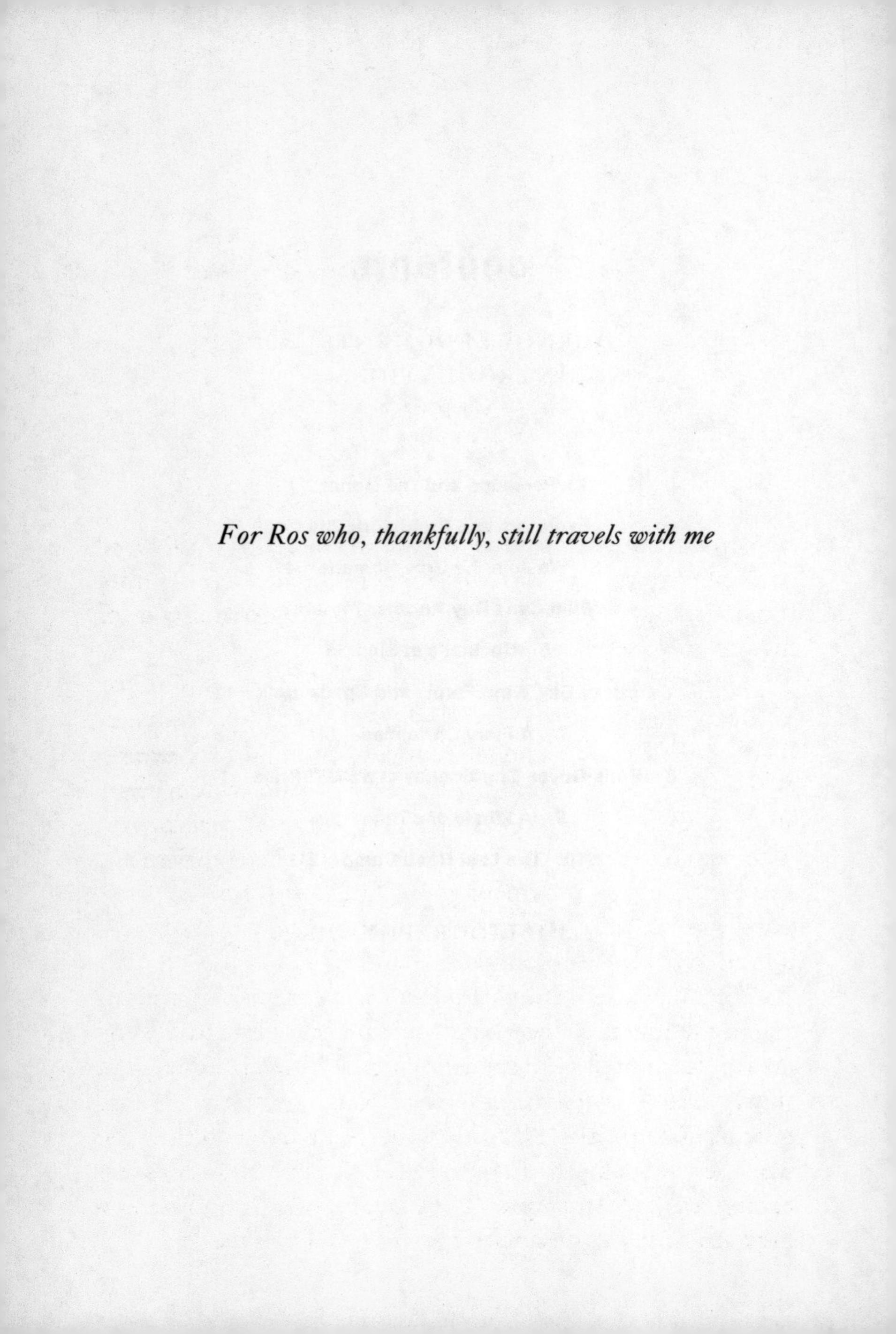

For Ros who, thankfully, still travels with me

Acknowledgments

Books are a team effort. Without my wife Ros, this one certainly would not have happened. Apart from sharing the journey, she researched and uncovered nuggets of history and photographed our progress.

Along the way we met Heather Messer and Greg Williams, and their two boys Todd and Ryan, who share our love of wild places and do a much better job of seeing them. They have been on the road now for three years, and have no plans to stop. Our chance meeting at Thomas River, Cape Arid National Park, in Western Australia, led to a firm ongoing friendship and I thank Greg for allowing some of his professional landscape photography to be included.

We met many delightful people in camping grounds and in the middle of nowhere—not all 'grey nomads' by any means. It is not only the retired brigade who are circulating slowly around Australia's enormous coastline. Young people, mostly with less time available on the road than the wrinklies, are camping from the boot of their hatchbacks and having a wonderful time. They even give the impression they are happy to chat with grey nomads like us.

Our stay with Patty and Russell Leighton at their property within sight of the Stirling Ranges reinforced a friendship Ros began when she interviewed Patty for a book published in 1995 by the ABC to celebrate its 'Women of the Land' award.

Les Bail, who manages Whaleworld in Albany, and his wife Dorothy were superb hosts and generous with source material. Denis Horgan, founder of Leeuwin Estate, and winemaker Bob Cartwright were so welcoming and hospitable that memories of our visit are clouded in a vinous haze—after having sampled many delicious wines of great depth and beauty from that well-favoured district. I thank you Denis for later information sent to me about the Margaret River district, and for correcting inaccuracies in stories imperfectly recalled from my vineyard visit.

Thanks also to the Adelaide *Advertiser* for permission to publish two news articles on a certain unforgettable theatrical event in Barmera (1972) and Bronwell Hurrell's vivid report on galah culling in Port Lincoln (1997); and to ABC Books for an excerpt from Bill Bunbury's interview with former Western Australia forester, Jack Tompson, in *Voices From a Vanishing Australia* edited by Nina Riemer.

Patrick Gallagher, publisher of Allen & Unwin, did not blanch when the idea of this book was sprung on him out of the blue, even though I was contracted to write one on an entirely different subject. Nina Riemer has edited six of my seven published books, and undertook her now well-tuned role of sounding-board, elegant stylist and gentle persuader in reigning me back from occasional vulgar excesses. Ros's aunt Nora Bonney, who maintains she can think of no more joyous task than copy-reading manuscripts, did so out of the goodness of her heart, with her usual passion for attempting to safeguard the basics of the English language from colloquial assaults. And Hank Nelson remains a good man for a title. Allen & Unwin's senior editor Rebecca Kaiser is somehow ever-cheerful whenever contacted about anything. I thank her, and the designer, Nada Backovic. I have been fortunate to work with the 'dream team' of publishing.

Introduction

I know of no more pleasant prospect than setting off on a driving and camping holiday in Australia—in the knowledge that there is enough time available to stay an extra day or two in a pleasant spot if that seems a good idea, or perhaps change plans quite radically on a whim and head off in unexpected directions.

Such freedom of choice is rare in busy lives. I managed it first in 1974, when I had been at the ABC long enough to qualify for some long-service leave. With my wife Ros and then 18-month-old son Barnaby, we set to go off halfway around Australia for six months in a battered 1967-vintage VW Kombi, towing a trailer. I had not experienced the incomparable pleasure of sleeping out without a tent under the blazing stars of an outback Australian sky, after a delectable damper had risen and browned in a camp oven on the coals of a dying fire. Such pleasures can be and are taken for granted by many knowledgeable Australians, but those who have lived in other countries know well how extremely fortunate we are to have the space, beauty, availability and safety of our 'wide brown land'.

As we headed across the Barkly Tablelands from

Queensland towards Three Ways in the Northern Territory more than a quarter of a century ago, Ros and I discussed whether we had time to go north to Darwin, or whether we should turn left at Three Ways and begin to head home, down the unsealed red-dust Stuart Highway, to the south coast. We decided to head home. But when we came within range of ABC Tennant Creek radio, we heard there had been heavy rain in the Centre, and that tourist coaches were bogged and stranded at Ayers Rock. I can still recall the delicious, almost irresponsible joy of saying to Ros: 'Bugger it, let's go north to Darwin anyway'. The freedom to make such cavalier decisions is rare, and we did turn right and drove to Darwin, and left, fortunately, shortly before the city was blown away by Cyclone Tracy.

Our journey up the east coast, across to the Northern Territory, and down through the red centre via the Oodnadatta Track to Adelaide and back to Sydney, was one of life's great experiences. Mercifully Ros and I share a love of camping and remote places and we managed an occasional camping excursion while our two boys were growing up, taking them away from school sometimes with their teachers' blessing. 'They will learn more on the road out there than they will here for those extra few weeks.'

But it was not until the late 1990s that Ros and I were free from family and work responsibilities to travel again with enough time available to develop that sense of liberation and appreciation of space and place.

Our aim was a coastal journey—or as close to it as we could—from South Australia, across the Nullarbor, to the south-west of Western Australia. It was not a journey either of us had done before, and it was also a personal rediscovery of the comparatively recent history of this country.

At school in the 1940s and '50s I had been given the usual dose of what passed then for history. It was rather like taking cod-liver oil, which was also inflicted on my generation. When we weren't learning irrelevant lists of Pommy Kings and Queens, we were getting rudimentary accounts of early Australian explorers, like Blaxland, Lawson and Wentworth, who were said to be the first to cross the Blue Mountains. They were not, as has been realised subsequently. But W C Wentworth lived a long life, and assiduously worked on his own myth. It didn't matter whether the names were Stuart, Sturt, Gosse, Kennedy, Eyre or Leichhardt—the bare bones of their achievements and failures were catalogued and force-fed to us in class. It was like learning slabs of the telephone book.

History often comes alive, however, when you cover the same ground as the pioneers—albeit in greater comfort. When Ros and I stood on the cliffs of the Great Australian Bight we had the experiences of two explorers on which to reflect. Matthew Flinders, who in 1802 was in some mild despair navigating his way on the seaward side of those same cliffs, complained in his log that not only did there seem to be no hint of any kind of entrance to the inland sea that geographers of the day felt must be in the centre of Australia, but the cliffs were so uniform that he found it difficult to sketch and plot their outline on his charts.

Almost 40 years later, Edward John Eyre, his overseer Baxter and three Aboriginal companions were walking their horses along the top of these same porous limestone cliffs wondering how long they could last before they died of thirst. Eyre, unlike other European explorers of his day, not only got on well with Aboriginal people but realised how important their local knowledge was in locating bush tucker and water. But he had been told by the last tribe he had contact with near the head of the Bight, that they knew of no water to the west where he was determined to travel. Obsession, bravery, foolishness, or a combination of all these? Certainly a remarkable sense of destiny in a 24 year old that was eventually fulfilled.

Ros and I found ourselves reading avidly of the experiences of the pioneer explorers as we drove west. Eyre's journey came to life as we combined following his route (roughly) while having access to much more entertaining accounts of his life than were available to me at school. The further west we went, the more rich the panoply of early navigators. French names on the coast went back to voyages of explorers like Baudin and D'Entrecasteaux—and Dutch-named features like the Nuyts Archipelago took us back to the seventeenth century. No wonder Western Australians become bored with the notion that Australia's European history began with Captain James Cook's voyage up the east coast of Australia in the late-eighteenth century.

I kept a diary of our two-month odyssey to the west but had not considered writing a book—until we returned to Sydney. The notion of describing our modest journey in the context of early European explorers came after we had talked about our experiences with friends—who were particularly fascinated to hear aspects of Eyre's extraordinary year-long exploratory journey from South Australia to King George Sound in Western Australia. His journey has most aspects of a good story including murder, near-death through thirst, and salvation from the sea at the most unlikely moment. 'Why don't you write a book about it', my friends kept saying.

So I did.

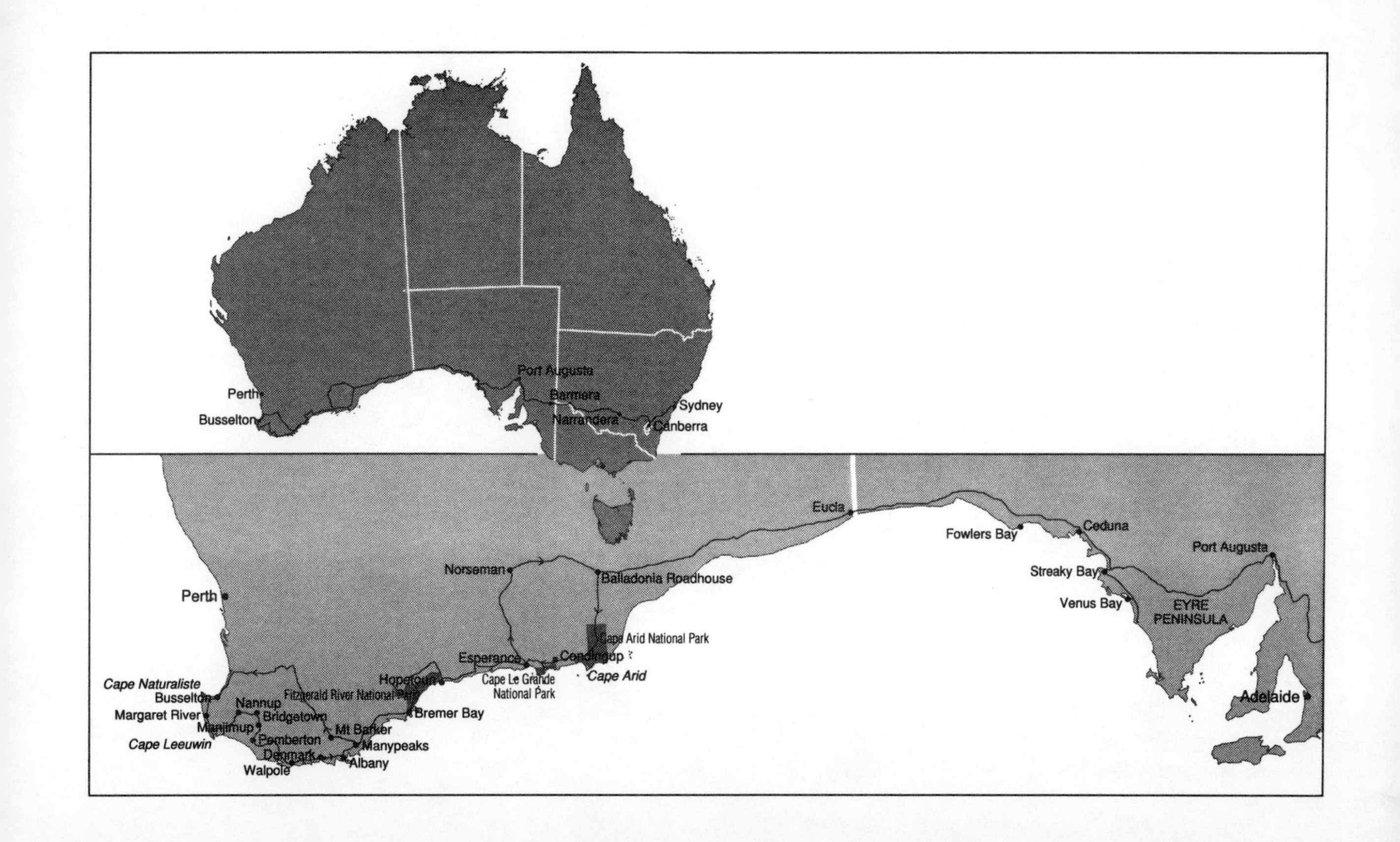

Perth
Busselton
Port Augusta
Barmera
Narrandera
Sydney
Canberra
Eucla
Fowlers Bay
Ceduna
Port Augusta
Norseman
Balladonia Roadhouse
Perth
Streaky Bay
Venus Bay
EYRE PENINSULA
Cape Arid National Park
Esperance
Condingup
Cape Arid
Cape Le Grande National Park
Hopetoun
Cape Naturaliste
Busselton
Nannup
Fitzgerald River National Park
Margaret River
Bridgetown
Bremer Bay
Manjimup
Mt Barker
Cape Leeuwin
Pemberton
Manypeaks
Denmark
Albany
Walpole
Adelaide

one

Penelope and The Manor

'Look—it's a dunny in a tree!'

Well, it was on a fence post actually. Heading west from Ceduna towards the Western Australian border on the Eyre Highway you begin to run out of barbed wire as the last of the parched, marginal sheep country gives way to unfenced mallee scrub, and then to open saltbush plains with no trees at all—the true Nullarbor Plain.

Ros had spotted it. I was driving Penelope, lost in my thoughts and semi-hypnotised by the dead-straight ribbon of bitumen ahead.

'Are you sure?'

'Yes!'

'Can't be.'

Ros was cocky. 'Bet you five bucks.'

We were about two kilometres on by then, with Penelope towing The Manor at our steady cruising speed of 100 kilometres per hour. The road was clear fore and aft, and I slowed down, did a U-turn and headed back. There had to be a photograph in it at least.

And there it was—a ceramic toilet bowl perched

perkily on a fence post, nicely offset by a photogenic dead mallee branch. Perhaps it had fallen off the proverbial truck? Or had some mad surrealist artist taken it out there as a free-form outback sculpture? One of life's little unexplained mysteries, really. A travel vignette on which to ponder.

We are heading west in early December, but it is unseasonably cool. A week ago it had been 45° Celsius at Ceduna. Not the most sensible time of the year for outback travel, but we are squeezed into university holidays because of Ros's horticulture course. I have promised to stop using the old Dorothy Parker line: 'You can lead a whore-to-culture, but you can't make her think.' Not that Ros was offended by it, just bored by repetition. I do tend to overwork my best lines even when they are someone else's.

We have two months to explore the southern coastline and south-west corner of Western Australia—which we hope will not be a furnace—and return to Sydney. First we will follow the route that the explorer Edward John Eyre took in 1840, around the Great Australian Bight from South Australia to King George Sound in Western Australia. We think of Edward John as we sit in air-conditioned comfort looking at the waterless, relentless mallee-dotted landscape that nearly killed him and his party. Behind us rolls The Manor, 60 litres of water in her tank, all mod cons, plenty of tucker and comfortable beds waiting for us at the end of each day.

Our choice of camper is a Jayco Flight, the smallest of the range, which collapses down into a trailer for easy towing. At the end of the day you wind it up with a crank handle, pull beds out at each end, and the whole thing expands miraculously like Dr Who's Tardis. Inside are a stove, fridge, two bench seats and a table. We fell in love with it at a caravan and camping show where we intended just to look. Ten minutes later (it seemed) we were signing up for a new one. Ros thought it was such a luxurious way to camp that she instantly christened it The Manor.

'OK', I said, sensing as one often does in a relationship that the decision was final, 'but what about the Toyota Landcruiser?'

'Penelope', said Ros triumphantly. (For those who may not watch the ABC she was referring to a long-running comedy series called *To the Manor Born*, which starred the formidable Penelope Keith and Peter Bowles.) I twigged the connection quickly enough. 'But Ros, we simply can't have a four-wheel drive called Penelope!'

'Why not?'

'What about my macho outback image? People might find out . . .'

'You haven't got one anyway.'

Penelope and The Manor it was.

We made some slight amendments to the basics of the Jayco. We ordered the off-road model, with higher clearance and a more robust chassis, and asked for wheels to match those on the Toyota. The idea of this is to have interchangeable wheels in case of an emergency. Mind you, Toyota Landcruisers have their spare wheel suspended under the rear of the vehicle, making it so difficult to get at that mechanically challenged people like me might be forced to sell the car to avoid changing the wheel. At least, I thought, we could filch the spare tyre off the back of The Manor first, before facing up to salvaging Penelope's spare in the unlikely (but not impossible) event of having two punctures on the same day. The bigger wheels on The Manor gave us an extra ten centimetres' clearance, but meant that the spare had to be mounted behind the back bumper bar, and not sandwiched between the bar and the trailer body.

Now those who muck about with well-established designs do so at their peril. And I mean peril, as we were to find out soon enough. We had two jerry-can holders welded on to the back bumper of The Manor for extra water and diesel.

Penelope was a 1994 ex-government vehicle which meant it had two barn doors that opened out at the back, rather than the upward-opening hatch of the non-commercial Landcruisers. We felt good about her right from the start. She had a diesel engine, which we wanted for economy and pulling power, had only 44 000 kilometres on the clock, and seemed in mint condition. These basic models have no frills like central locking or carpets. Penelope did, though, have power steering and airconditioning, a bull bar and an impressive-looking winch. We acquired her from a dealer in Launceston after she had been bought at auction in Sydney by a Tasmanian firm specialising in rural industries. According to the dealer who sold her to us, the original buyers had paid too much. Penelope sat on their showroom floor for a year, in a sense waiting for us. In order to get a sale, the original buyers tarted her up by adding fancy aluminium wheels, wide tyres, and blue stripes along her sparkling white flanks. On 30 June (last day of the tax year) my canny dealer made them an offer they chose not to refuse, and then passed on Penelope to the Bowdens for a most reasonable price.

To prepare for our journey west, we had some sliding drawers with compartments built into Penelope's rear section and a cargo barrier installed. We took the back seat out and fitted some big white polymer storage bins for our supplies. The Bowdens have always believed that camping is not about deprivation, but indulgence. In our first major journey halfway around Australia in a battered VW Kombi 28 years ago, we actually had a spice-rack built by Ros into the side door. As I said to her at the time, 'All wok and no play makes a dull cook'.

We carried the spices less obviously this time, but they and the wok were there. The sliding drawers at the back held heavy equipment like an extra jack, tools, spare engine hoses and belts, ropes, extra engine oil, an axe, bush saw, a folding barbecue plate, and the winding handles needed to erect The Manor. The advantage of these drawers was that you could open them without disturbing the rest of the load, which also included a portable fridge to complement the one in The Manor. A second battery was added to power such accessories, and a compressor to pump up tyres in the boondocks. Two folding tables and chairs were positioned behind the front seats so they were easy to take out for lunch stops. We avoided having a roof-rack to lessen drag. In any case, the experts say it is much better to keep the centre of gravity as low as possible with four-wheel-drive vehicles.

Planning all this, and hoping it works, is half the fun. On the road or in camping areas it is a constant joy to eye off other travellers' rigs to see how they do it, purloin good ideas, or simply comfort yourself that your system is better than theirs.

I have a holiday song, associated with the freedom of setting out on long journeys where you don't have a strict schedule and you might stay a day somewhere or you might stay two. Or you might decide to go somewhere in the morning, and then turn left instead of right and change your mind—liberation from the tight, structured, arranged lives we lead in cities. The song is 'Everybody's Talkin', sung by Harry Nilsson. I think it featured in the film *Midnight Cowboy* when the hustler, played by Jon Voight, and his crippled friend (Dustin Hoffman) set off in a Greyhound bus from a grey New York for sunny Florida and a new life.

Perhaps there is a certain 1960s nostalgia built in too. I played it when we headed north in 1974 for a six-month odyssey (with our then 18-month-old son Barnaby) up the east coast, across to Darwin, and down the red dust of the Stuart Highway, the Oodnadatta Track, to Adelaide and back to Sydney. More than a quarter of a century later I found the song on a CD and dubbed it over and over again on the one tape, so I could play it at will. Ros called it my morning prayers.

I played it loudly on 4 December, singing along joyously as we headed out of Sydney on the Hume Highway for Canberra. The inevitable hassles of shucking off city life for the road had been conquered at last, and I was seized by a fierce feeling of exhilaration which quickly turned to stark terror. As I began to overtake a semitrailer, The Manor—well-behaved until that critical moment—began to rock 'n' roll alarmingly at 110 kph. Now I had been told that if such a thing happened, the drill was to operate the electric brakes on the towed vehicle manually, and accelerate to straighten things out. I did not do this. In fact I'm not sure what I did, but I let the semitrailer driver have all the road he wanted, and managed to drop back, get into the left lane, and slow the gyrating Manor down until I could safely stop beside the expressway.

Harry Nilsson was still singing away—cheerfully oblivious of our imminent demise. I switched off the tape, the engine, and had an attack of the retrospective shudders. It would have been a great start, wiping us out in the first hour of a two-month voyage. But what on earth was happening? My tyre pressures were impeccable. I'd checked them before I left. All the tyres were brand new anyway. Everything was new.

There was another possibility. It is essential that the balance of a trailer, caravan or boat that you are towing be nose-heavy for stability. Perhaps, in the final packing, we had upset this balance and become nose-light. One test is to take off the trailer, and see if you can lift its weight in the horizontal, towing position. If you can, it's too light. With heavy traffic whoomphing past at 100-plus knots and unnerving proximity, I pulled on the trailer's handbrake, connected the jogger wheel and disconnected The Manor from the towing ball and safety chains. Sure enough, I could lift the front of the whole trailer up easily with one hand!

I connected up again, and joined Ros in the front seat. 'It's out of balance. We'll have to take it back to Jayco and get something done about it. See if there is an agency in Canberra.'

As it happened, there wasn't, but mercifully there was one listed in Queanbeyan, in nearby New South Wales.

We were not in a position to go back to Sydney. It was already 3 pm and I was due to front at the High Court in Canberra in four hours' time. Not before the learned judges actually, but as an after-dinner speaker to an audience of doctors. (The ground floor of the nation's supreme law-making court can be hired for private functions.) We decided to press on—cautiously. But not too slowly, or we wouldn't make the dinner.

Exhilaration had transmogrified to worry and anxiety. Not only that, Penelope seemed to have lost her oomph. I could barely coax her to pull The Manor at more than 80 kph. After 20 kilometres of sluggish travel, a smell of burning caused me to stop and check. Penelope had been doing very well to pull The Manor at any speed because in my addled state beside the road I had neglected to release the handbrake on the trailer wheels. The brake drums were red hot, and smoking.

Now at this stage I thought I was doing really well. An out-of-balance camper with burnt-out brakes and possibly also wheel bearings. And all this achieved in the first two hours!

The first priority was to get to our hotel and change, so I could do my number at the High Court. At least The Manor's wheels were still turning, and strangely enough she seemed to tow much more easily with the brakes off. Like the Battle of Waterloo, it was 'a close run thing', but we managed to amble through the front door of the High Court on time, suitably booted and spurred, and trying to look comfortable and relaxed, as Prime Minister John Howard no doubt would wish us to be in the national capital, and indeed all the time.

The dinner was hosted by a pharmaceutical firm

anxious to extol the virtues of a new cholesterol and blood pressure reducing drug it had developed that, it was said, had no measurable side effects. Not only did it give years of added useful life, but I seem to recall it also enhanced sexual performance and curled your hair. So enthusiastic were the pitch and presentation of those peddling the stuff that one of the medicos at our table interjected loudly: 'If it's that good, why don't you just add it to the water?' After our experiences on the highway a few hours earlier I could have done with a good slug of it myself for all those reasons.

We were put up in some style at the Hotel Kurrajong, sparing a thought for Prime Minister Ben Chifley who lived there while he was in Canberra for parliamentary sessions. Chif had to walk down the hallway in his dressing-gown and slippers to a communal toilet and bathroom. We had an en suite. The hotel—only a few minutes' walk from Old Parliament House and the High Court—has been extensively and expensively modernised, with a discerning eye to its heritage. Fragments of the original wallpaper were discovered and copied, including the ornate friezes running around the lobby wall at picture rail height. There is a remarkable photograph behind the reception desk showing the original hotel circa 1929 on its own in the middle of an empty paddock.

First thing next morning we rang the Jayco agents in Queanbeyan, explained our predicament and a comfortable and relaxed Noel McAlister suggested we come straight out to see them. We were there by 10.30 and they could not have been more helpful. Mechanics Tony and John dropped the job they were doing for someone else and had the wheels off The Manor in their workshop almost before Ros and I had scrambled out of Penelope's front seats. The good news was I had not burnt out the wheel bearings with my idiotic performance with the handbrake, although the friction from the brake drums had blistered the paint on the hubs.

Then they scratched their heads about why The Manor was nose-heavy. It was all quite simple when it was explained. A bit like two kids on a seesaw, said Tony. 'If there is a big fat kid on one end and a skinny kid on the other, the skinny kid only has to move backwards quite a short distance to balance up.' The villain in this case was the larger and heavier spare wheel I had insisted on, which had been mounted behind the back bumper because there was no room between the bar and the back of the trailer body. That, plus the jerry cans of water and fuel, had unbalanced the seesaw. The obvious solution was to mount the spare on the front draw-bars of The Manor—except that there were already two gas bottles taking up the space. Tony and John whipped out their tape measures, did a quick calculation and disappeared behind a flurry of sparks with their heavy-duty angle grinders.

For someone as technically challenged as I am, it is inspirational to watch two blokes who know what they are doing bend metal to their collective will. Within three hours of our driving in the gate, they had the brakes relined, bearings repacked and greased, electric brakes adjusted, gas-bottle brackets moved back, rewelded, and the spare wheel mounted tidily in front of them. A squirt or two of silver paint from a pressure pack, and it was better than new. Somehow it only cost $164! How that could be, with two men working for three hours I knew not, but we were exceedingly grateful. So by lunchtime we were heading west, with a properly balanced rig, in high spirits, with Harry Nilsson on the tape player once again exhorting us onward to coastal sunshine, sweetness and light. Such a situation had not seemed remotely possible at breakfast time. We continued to have fond thoughts of the Jayco Queanbeyan lot, and made a vow to send them jolly post-cards from faraway places with strange-sounding names in the weeks ahead.

Even if I had not needed to come to Canberra for my brief High Court appearance, we would have chosen that route to get clear of the Sydney basin and navigate over the Great Dividing Range with the minimum of effort and fuel. The alternative would have been to grind our way slowly over the Blue Mountains via Penrith and Katoomba on the Great Western Highway from Sydney. Or take the narrower Bells Line of Road to Lithgow, undeniably spectacular, but slow going when you are towing a heavy trailer up and down that roller-coaster, ridge-hugging route through the mountains.

It was not long after the first settlement in Port Jackson in 1788 that the early residents realised that the shortage of available land in the Sydney basin would put gross limitations on the pastoral ambitions of the new colony. But the oft-told saga of breaking through the Blue Mountains to the 'vision splendid and the sunlit plains extended' has been a wonderful exercise in historical myth-making. As all schoolchildren of my generation were taught relentlessly, the honours went to 'The Three Explorers', Blaxland, Lawson and Wentworth who, we were told, were the first to blaze a trail across the Blue Mountains in 1813. In fact they did not make it right across, as the 'beauteous landscape' they gazed upon from their vantage point of Mount York was not over the Bathurst plains, but only into Cox's Valley which, admittedly, had potential for grazing cattle, but was well and truly bounded by lots more Blue Mountains.

Overlooking the fact (as white historians generally did) that the Aborigines had been happily ambling backwards and forwards through the Blue Mountains for umpteen thousands of years, there is pretty conclusive evidence that the first European-influenced crossing took place as early as 1789. It's difficult to put an exact date on it, because the expeditioners were the four intrepid cows and two bulls (and their progeny) which escaped from Sydney Cove in the first year of settlement. They weren't silly enough to try and clamber through the gorges, valleys and sandstone cliffs of the Blue Mountains. They simply ambled down towards Goulburn and munched their way west over pastures and low hills where the Blue Mountains cease to be a serious impediment to the west—which is exactly what Ros and I were doing with Penelope and The Manor.

(In April 1998 I heard on ABC Radio that distinctively horned, direct descendants of these robust early explorers were still to be found in remote valleys on the western side of the Blue Mountains, and that they should be hunted down and shot to protect the blood lines of modern cattle. Historical conservationists were arguing for their preservation and DNA testing to see whether they could be traced back to first settlement.)

The list of explorers who roamed about in the Blue Mountains before Blaxland, Lawson and Wentworth did their bit in 1813 was extensive, and included Dawes, Tench, Paterson, Hacking, Everingham, Bass, Wilson,

Barrallier and Caley—a process of discovery of which 'The Three Explorers' were the ultimate beneficiaries. (By the way, a fascinating account of the history of Blue Mountains exploration can be read in *The Blue Mountains Rediscovered—Beyond the Myths of Early Australian Exploration* by Chris Cunningham, Kangaroo Press, 1996.)

Mind you, W C Wentworth did his best to foster his own legend through a long life and his own publishing ventures, which included the *Sydney Gazette* and *The Australian*, founded by Wentworth himself in 1824, which was a kind of early version of Dick Smith's *Australian Geographic*. These white, middle-class adventurers were also useful symbols of national pride against the background of the Boer War, the First World War, and Gallipoli. 'The Three Explorers' myth became unstoppable. How about this, from the pen of Stephen H Roberts in 1935:

> The distant ranges seemed so tranquilly blue as if to emphasise the death of attrition they were forcing on the colony . . . At last in May 1813, three youths . . . broke through the ramparts . . . through the starkness of the gorges (like the remains of some dreadful earthquake) . . . they pushed to a point where they finally looked down on the west—and in a moment extended the colony's outlook from the mountains to the farthest hazy horizon where the plains stretched out in the sepia mist.

Ripping yarns, what? And Blaxland, Lawson and Wentworth didn't even get right through the mountains anyway. I say let's hear it for the First Fleet cattle, who most likely first found their way through the natural corridor to the west.

Our own plans were to take the Sturt Highway from

Gundagai to Narrandera and across the Hay plains to Mildura and then make a beeline for Port Augusta to begin our crossing of the Eyre Peninsula. (Charles Sturt and Edward John Eyre were contemporaries and friends, and both excelled at driving cattle across unknown country in the 1830s.)

We weren't planning to camp in The Manor until after Port Augusta. The idea was not to linger in New South Wales on this part of the trip, because of time constraints, but to begin our journey to the west (proper) as close as possible to Eyre's 1840 exploratory push from the peninsula named after him, around the head of the Bight, to King George Sound (where Albany now is), keeping as close to the coast as practicable.

Because of our delayed exit from Canberra, we were happy to make it to Narrandera by dusk, checking into one of the many excellent, economical motels in the town. It was hot, with the mercury still around 30° Celsius. Electing for Chinese takeaway I went looking for a cold bottle of beer, and found myself having a surreal experience. The pub, in the centre of town, was admittedly small. It had cold beer on tap, but none in bottles. Nor did it sell any wine at all, hot or cold. 'Oh it's a terrible place, the pub with hot beer.'

Australians are lucky with their motels. It is taken for granted that you can make yourself a cup of tea, with electric jug and all the doings supplied—even complimentary biscuits. The bed in our motel was firm and comfortable, and even the shower was generous, in a bathroom in which a medium-sized cat could be safely swung, should that have been necessary. The airconditioner roared like a DC3 aero engine warming up, but at least there was one.

Narrandera is on the Murrumbidgee, and on our way out the next morning we doubled back briefly to have a look out over the Narrandera lake in the early-morning light. At the turn of the century the Murrumbidgee Irrigation Authority was a major employer, constructing canals to carry precious water to the new irrigated farms. The lake did not exist until 1925, and then only by accident. During the severe floods in May of that year, two small boys drilled a tiny hole into the main canal bank to see what sort of flow they could get. As it happened they got a good one. By the next day that section of the canal bank had collapsed, and the whole of the Bundidgerry flat was flooded. Bill Talbot, the town clerk of the day, suggested to the council that the flooded area be developed as a bathing and recreation area. It was named Lake Talbot in 1950—without a plaque to the anonymous urchins who were really responsible.

It was going to be another hot one as we headed west across the Hay plains—a cloudless, beautiful morning but with an ominous haze of bushfire smoke on the horizon. The lush green crops of the paddocks that were irrigated was a startling contrast to the white, parched grass of those that were not. After Hay, the country becomes flatter and featureless, with almost bare earth and stunted scrub seemingly stretching to infinity. The bitumen ribbon ahead was a shimmering mirage out of which huge trucks appeared, their tops seemingly detached by optical illusion, dominating the landscape in the absence of any trees. We passed the entrance to a property on our right appropriately named 'Hell's Gates'.

There was some shade under peppertrees near a rather desolate artificial irrigation lake close to Euston.

We stationed ourselves comfortably with our folding table and chairs and watched pelicans paddle solemnly by as we hoed into fresh bread sandwiches bulging with corned beef and pickle. Stupidly I left our portable cold pack on the trailer bar, but it sat there rather miraculously without falling off. I noticed it when we swapped over the driving just past the South Australian border. We are developing a routine of driving for two hours each to minimise driver fatigue. One of the advantages of a camping rig like The Manor, which tows as a low trailer rather than a caravan, is that you can cover long distances quickly when you want to.

The quarantine inspection on the border of South Australia and New South Wales was rigorous. But we were able to stock up with wonderful fresh fruit in Renmark from a roadside stall staffed by a cheerful Italian woman with only rudimentary English. Her family has probably been living in this area for generations. She insisted we sample her peaches, nectarines, apricots and even fresh figs.

I was intrigued to hear on ABC radio that the weather forecast for that evening included a warning to farmers to expect downy mildew as well as showers and storms. Does the mildew fall like rain? And what on earth are the farmers supposed to do about it apart from curse?

Our next stop is Barmera, by Lake Bonney. And we will erect The Manor, and not stay in a motel. What is the point of having plans if you don't change them? There are two Lake Bonneys in South Australia, both named after Ros's great-great-grandfather, the explorer Charles Bonney and she is keen to investigate her ancestral connections.

I have a different interest in Barmera but it also has a

Bonney link. Many years ago a friend in Adelaide sent me a priceless cutting from the *Advertiser* newspaper about a cultural event that took place in the Bonney Theatre in August 1978. Sure enough, there it was as we drove towards the lake-side camping ground. The story, in my view, was a minor classic and needs to be shared. It was headlined 'THE TIME TRUE ART CAME TO BARMERA':

> A 'tucker' truck missed its cue at a theatre banquet in Barmera on Friday—and brought down the house.
>
> The 280 guests at the Bonney Theatre, out for an evening of wining and dining and music-hall style entertainment, sipped on their pre-dinner drinks, unaware of the fate of the truck bringing the banquet.
>
> Four hours later they were still sipping away—with disastrous consequences.
>
> First of all, the truck bringing the food from Adelaide had a series of flat tyres. Then the trailer was damaged, spoiling the food.
>
> Back in the Bonney Theatre the evening organised by the Apex Club went on regardless.
>
> A play, 'A Bard's Banquet', with players from the Arts Council of South Australia, was delayed to keep the acts in time with the scheduled banquet—but by 9 pm, with still no sign of the food, the curtain went up.
>
> According to the Arts Council touring manager Mr J Maxwell, the famished but lubricated crowd was rowdy, somewhat unruly, and beyond caring for the finer points of theatre.
>
> An organiser mounted the centre stage to appeal for order, but was hit on the neck by a tomato. One of the audience quipped that the tomato should have been shared by the hungry audience.
>
> Soup, hurriedly rustled up on the spot, was served soon after,

but when empty, the soup plates were hurled about the hall.

Mr Maxwell described the evening as 'a nightmare happening before my eyes'. He said the climax came when his cast left the stage and reported seeing an over-amorous couple staging its own performance in the gallery overlooking the audience.

A second couple was later seen having 'intercourse between courses'.

'It gave everyone something other than hunger to talk about', Barmera resident and one of the guests Mrs C Rooney, said last night.

The caterer finally arrived at 11 pm. Some of the food was promptly eaten, while the rest was disposed of as projectiles aimed at the actors on the stage.

The caterers did not charge. The guests had paid $9. Drinks were extra. The St John Ambulance Brigade got about $2000 from the epic fund-raiser.

'I'm just grateful that my actors got through the night relatively unscathed', the Arts Council Manager Mr Maxwell said.

two

Explorers and Prehistoric Ants

The woman who booked us into the Lake Bonney Holiday Park was extremely cheerful. Where were we from? Where were we going? How long had we been on the road? She seemed genuinely interested. Yet we must have been the umpteenth visitors with whom she has had the same conversation. How could she possibly maintain this friendly engagement with the public? I could see myself becoming the Basil Fawlty of Lake Bonney if I were running the place, grumpily handing over toilet-block keys to visitors and fuming about teenagers standing under the hot showers for all eternity. Perhaps her pleasantness was sustained by the beauty of the park.

Among the camping alternatives on offer at Barmera was the Pelican Point Nudist Resort. We were not tempted. Putting up The Manor for the first time on this expedition was going to be challenge enough without having to worry about protecting our own wobbly bits.

With familiarity born of practice, we will soon be able to do this without the need to exchange a word, in under ten minutes. On this occasion there is a lack of coordination.

The roof and canvas sidewalls have to be cranked up with a winding handle. The two beds are then pulled out and supported from the outside by metal struts. The sink and stove top, hinged and folded over to lower the towing profile, are resurrected. The door, its upper section cunningly secured to the ceiling inside, has to be unhooked and connected to its lower half. I am distracted by the views over the lake, and forget to wind the stabilisers down. Ros, wrestling with the door inside, testily inquires what the hell I am doing out there.

There are thundery showers forecast, and we decide to unfurl the awning. This is best done *before* winding The Manor up to its full height. I teeter on the top step of a small ladder fighting with spring-loaded support poles. Profanity floats across the lake and the white cockies jeer at me from the treetops. We can do better than this and we will. It has been a long day. Ros liberates two welcome cold and soothing ales from Penelope's fridge. We ignore the time change that makes it a rather premature evening drinkies time of 5 and not 5.30 pm. We usually try and hold out till 6.

We are camped on grass beside the lake, under gum trees clustered with larrikin white cockatoos which, for seemingly no reason, suddenly all take off and wheel about above us screeching in their usual ear-splitting way. They make the smaller clusters of pink-and-grey galahs sound quite pianissimo. Pelicans paddle past the shoreline with stately unhurried calm, and the magpies' mellifluous warbling calls can hardly be heard against the competition. Flocks of other waterbirds can be seen in the distance across the lake to the west.

Ros reminds me that this is a re-run of the arrival of her

great-great-grandfather Charles Bonney and his companion Joseph Hawdon when they came upon the lake in 1838. They were droving cattle from New South Wales to Adelaide—the first time this had been attempted. Hawdon noted in his diary 'a fine lake of fresh water, about thirty miles in circumference', beside which they camped. Like us, they arrived in the evening. They noticed some Aborigines camped further around the lake who were also aware of them. It was a beautiful moonlit night, and the two men strolled along the banks to shoot some of the thousands of ducks resting on the water. It had a spectacular effect, as the echoes of the shots 'rolled along the water magnificently—one would have supposed that a hundred shots had been fired at the same moment'. At that point all the waterbirds took off 'screaming and cackling with alarm at the novel sound'.

I'll bet the Aborigines knew they were there after that!

Hawdon learned that the Aboriginal name for the lake was 'Nookamka', but on that same day named it Lake Bonney 'after my friend and fellow traveller Mr M C Bonney, whose company contributed so much to the pleasure of my expedition'.

When Ros told her aunt Nora Bonney about our intended journey, she said we would be passing Lake Bonney, which triggered Ros's interest in finding out more about her explorer great-great-grandfather. Like Edward John Eyre (with whom he was friendly) Bonney was an engaging young Englishman who arrived in Australia with the idea of making something of himself—and was sustained by a strong sense of adventure. Bonney was 21 when he arrived in New South Wales in 1834, first to work as a judge's clerk in Sydney, but his restless spirit soon had him working on a new pastoral property on the Murray River.

His employer, C H Ebden, asked him to try to find a practicable stock route to the new Port Phillip settlement, and after a couple of attempts he got through in 1837. At that time the Port Phillip Settlement (as it was called then) 'consisted of a few huts with one newly erected weatherboard store, conspicuous by its fresh coat of paint amongst the ruder habitations by which it was surrounded'. To get back to Sydney, Bonney first had to sail across Bass Strait to Launceston—from which city, of course, Melbourne had been settled. As a former Tasmanian, I think it important to remind Melburnians of this.

When Bonney got back to Sydney he set off south again with another mob of cattle—keeping a wary eye out for bushrangers—pioneering the route that he first called the 'Sydney Road' and is today known as the Hume Highway.

With the summer twilight stretching ahead, a proudly erected Manor and our beds ready for later use, we decided to explore and eat out at the historic Overland Corner Hotel beside the Murray River. Driving around the eastern shore of the lake we stopped by the ruined stone walls of another hotel, built in 1859 after Bonney and Hawdon had found a way through the complex waterways feeding the Murray. The information plaque reminded us that this was not exploration for exploration's sake, but hard-edged commercial pastoral opportunism. Charles Sturt and Edward John Eyre (contemporaries of Hawdon and Bonney) also first made their reputations as early Australian explorers by droving cattle into unknown country.

We found the Overland Corner Hotel some twelve kilometres further on. It's a delightful blend of National Trust property and local hostelry. Its small stone rooms and inner courtyard are stuffed with fascinating historical bric-a-brac. On the window ledge beside us in the bar are a couple of early irons. One was fairly basic, designed to be filled with hot coals or charcoal—it even had a little chimney built on the sharp end. But the other, more technologically advanced iron was quite alarming, with a metal bulb on the rear end surrounded by a primus mechanism, and powered by petroleum. I kept imagining all the catastrophes to garments and the users, and the inadvertent house fires that it must have ignited. Medallions for bravery should have been issued by the manufacturers to the housewives of the day who attempted to use it.

The Overland Corner Hotel was flooded almost to the roof as recently as 1956. The waterline high up on the wallpaper can be seen clearly. It's either a flood or a famine in outback Australia.

Our excellent steaks were washed down with equally delicious local South Australian red and our talk turned to Charles Bonney. After his early success in taking cattle overland to Port Phillip, Bonney had become an expert bushman and drover, and he jumped at the chance to join Joseph Hawdon in his plan to drive cattle from New South Wales to Adelaide in January 1838.

'He was very good at avoiding conflict with Aborigines', said Ros. 'He used to play his flute to help overcome difficult situations.'

'Really?'

This apparently unlikely tactic is confirmed in an account of his 1838 journey written by Joseph Hawdon, who was also adept at avoiding conflict. On 6 March, at the end of a hard day's droving, Hawdon stripped off and went down to the river to have a drink. As he came out of the water he was somewhat alarmed to see five Aborigines standing on the bank about 15 metres above him, leaning on their spears. Not sure of their intentions, Hawdon decided to clown his way out of trouble, and 'commenced a dance, as a little merriment will at any time drive all hostility from their minds'. Once he had picked up his guns 'which I had incautiously left on the side of the bank' he felt more in control of the situation.

Getting back to camp after his impromptu, pre-emptive pirouette, he found Charles Bonney had been approached by a larger group of Aborigines and was handling things in his own inimitable style by 'playing a few sweet airs on his flute by the river side' for an audience of about 40 fascinated warriors. Hawdon was very taken with this and—clearly a believer in the doctrine of 'the noble savage'—noted in his diary: 'I have often noticed that the finest-looking men are fondest of hearing the music . . .'

Ros recalled that the author Ernestine Hill described Charles Bonney as a 'pied piper of the woodland' because of his penchant for entertaining both blacks and whites with his flute, writing that 'many a time he won a battle before it began by raising a general laugh'.

'I think my great-great-grandfather sounds a very nice bloke', said Ros. 'He would have been a wonderful travelling companion.'

'For the moment,' I said, 'you'll have to make do with me'.

The first sight of white men and their horned beasts must have been an alarming and bizarre sight for the local tribes. Four days before the all-dancing all-musical encounter, Hawdon and Bonney faced at least 100 warriors, formed up in front of their women and children, who threatened the party with their spears and gestured that they should go away. The explorers and their cattle moved on, only to encounter another big, similarly feisty group of armed Aborigines blocking their way. Again humour saved the day, as the blacks surrounded the party with uncertain intentions.

One of the Aborigines asked Hawdon, with suitable pantomime, whether the heifers in the flock were the wives of the white men? There was much laughter.

But a little later things became tense again, and when a warrior raised his spear while Hawdon's back was turned, he was nearly shot by one of the stockmen. On this occasion the cattle saved the day. Nervous at being surrounded, they suddenly rushed: '... two of the beasts charging the Blacks right and left, who saved themselves from being gored only by their extreme agility.' Hawdon noted that the cattle were very sensitive to the presence of Aborigines. 'Long before they could catch sight of the Blacks they evidently knew of their approach by the smell, and would carry their heads erect in the air, and snort aloud.'

After they passed Lake Bonney the explorers had good reason to be grateful to two local Aborigines who acted as guides and saved the party many days of painful unnecessary travel. Bonney and Hawdon had to decide whether to drive their heavy drays along the river flats, or up on the cliffs which were often two or three hundred metres high. The river flats were firmer, but sometimes the explorers would come to a dead end on a bend in the river, where the river eroded into high cliffs. Bonney was amazed at the intelligence their Aboriginal guides displayed. 'Before they had been half a day with us they knew as well as we did where a dray could go and where it could not go; although they had never seen white men before they never once made a mistake as to when we could keep to the flats and when we must take the high land.'

Bonney and Hawdon reached Adelaide in early April. Like Melbourne at that time, what was to be 'the city of churches' was just a collection of basic wooden huts. The settlers were surprised and delighted—particularly at the arrival of the overlanded cattle. Up till that time they had been living 'almost exclusively on kangaroo flesh'.

Replete with our elegantly roasted bits of cattle from the Overland Corner Hotel, Ros and I drove back to camp exhilarated by a dramatic sunset offset by the clearing storm clouds that never quite made it to Lake Bonney. I needn't have put the bloody awning up anyway!

We were woken at 6 am by the shrieking and screeching of our resident colony of white cockatoos. They also shat on The Manor's roof. One of us has to go.

I couldn't resist taking a photo of the Bonney Theatre on the way out through the main street in memory of 'The Bard's Banquet'. We had walked down to the banks of the Murray River from the Overland Corner Hotel, but were irritated by not seeing enough of it from the road. On a whim we turned down towards it and crossed to the northern bank on the ferry at Waikerie en route to Lock 2—one of the six Murray River locks that regulate the river's long meandering journey to South Australia's Coorong coast. We were glad we did, dallying a while on the cool green lawns near the lock-keeper's cottage. Lazy fat catfish surfaced periodically in the contained soupy water of the lock itself, feeding on surface insects. Out in the river, pelicans, ducks, shags and other questing fowl, paddling vigorously against the current, were feeding in the churned up water on the down-river side of the weir. No boats came through, alas.

This 'Big River' country has wonderful contrasts. Paddocks yellow with dry grass sprawl beside hectare after hectare of luxuriant green vineyards and citrus orchards. How on earth can they pick all those grapes—it has to be done by hand—let alone prune the vines?

Locusts splattered on to the windscreen, and began to clog up Penelope's radiator as we headed towards Peterborough. If we are still ploughing through them tomorrow, we will have to rig up some kind of radiator protection. The locals make do with green shadecloth across their front grilles, or specially designed metal mesh panels. We refuelled at Morgan because we wanted to check on the status of a gravel road to Burra, and it's always reassuring to have full tanks off the beaten track. The German influence in this area of South Australia is reflected in the variety of sausages available. We bought some dehydrated beer sticks, but jibbed at some particularly unattractive black sausages labelled 'Bum-Burners'. They looked as though they had already passed through.

The weather is unsettled, with banks of black clouds building up on the western side of Spencer Gulf as we wind through Horrocks Pass before joining Highway One for the final run into Port Augusta. We will try a motel one more time before settling into a less frenetic travelling pattern. But our room can only be described as basic, and the management foolish enough to solicit comments. Ros noted that the bed is too small, mattress too bouncy, and the sheets and pillows reek of cigarette smoke.

It did rain in the night, and we woke to an overcast, drizzling morning—an uncharacteristic environment in which to visit Port Augusta's excellent Arid Lands Botanic Gardens, first established in 1984. As we parked Penelope there was a minor cloudburst and we ran into the visitors' centre with our rain jackets streaming. Still, even arid land plants need to have a drink occasionally. The visitors' centre is a smart modern building with rammed-earth walls, and the Gardens—we were told—are supported by the Western Mining Corporation as well as the South Australian Government and other sponsors. The Gardens are built on degraded land to illustrate how Australia's natural plant and animal species and their ecosystems can be recreated and restored. We waited for the rain to clear before inspecting the sodden 'arid' surrounds.

A bedraggled and unshaven young man approached. 'You're Tim Bowden, aren't you?' I pleaded guilty.

'I am A Nonymous, a friend of Mavis Frizzletit.'

Somehow it seemed appropriate to meet a friend of Mavis's on a sopping-wet day in an arid lands botanic garden. I first became aware of Mavis when hosting the ABC's viewer and listener reaction program *Backchat* in the late 1980s and early 1990s. We had a policy of not running unsigned letters, or those with obvious nom de plumes. So it was that I found myself in spirited correspondence with Mavis Frizzletit of Bonnell's Bay, New South Wales. When I commented on camera that there didn't seem to be many Frizzletits in the phone book and why didn't Mavis come clean about who she was, she wrote in again, most indignant about how outrageous it was for me to make jokes about other people's names. (In real life Ms Frizzletit is Jaye Smith, a psychiatric nurse.)

I learned that Mavis was no prude, and wrote in strong support of raunchy programming and breaches of good taste. Her first-ever letter to *Backchat* on Denis Potter's *The Singing Detective* was a sign of things to come:

> I am writing in regard to that LEWD little offering on Sunday night . . . This show has it ALL—nudity, sex, violence, obscene language, graphic close-ups of YUKKY diseases; in fact EVERYTHING that makes a show WORTH WATCHING. It's FAB!!

One year Mavis sent me an invitation to a party at the home of one Lord Blackall to witness the annual Frizzle Awards for those who had best transgressed the bounds of good taste. The recipients were presented with a golden dog turd mounted on a small plinth. I was unable to attend, but heard later that Aldo Nonymous was an award winner. Now it seemed we had met face to face.

Aldo (Greg Piper) is—like Mavis—a psychiatric nurse. Outside Mavis's fantasy life, he is also a Councillor of the city of Lake Macquarie in New South Wales, and a committed conservationist. The Councillor was unshaven and looked somewhat frazzled (frizzled?) as he had been on a two-week tour of the Northern Territory and South Australia sleeping out in his swag, beside his car. Temporary dryness was at least available in the Arid

Lands Botanic Garden visitors' centre. But he was cheerful and had unearthed his last clean T-shirt.

The rain had stopped while I was catching up with Mavis's latest adventures—she has launched herself into cyberspace and now has her own web site on the Internet. We farewelled Aldo and walked through some of the 200 hectares of the unusually damp arid lands display. There are wooden walkways to protect the sand and vegetation from the marching of many feet, and it is a fascinating place to see. Relatively little scientific research has been done on the flora of arid Australia, now realised to be of worldwide significance. The preservation of remnant local native vegetation was the first priority, and now arid zone plants from throughout Australia are being added.

The Gardens are bordered on the eastern flank by the steep cliffs of Spencer Gulf—at this point only a creek, bordered by mangroves. The great English navigator and explorer Matthew Flinders came here on 13 March 1802 and the realisation that the splendid gulf (or gulph, as he wrote) had petered out into a miserable swamp was a bitter disappointment. There was not even any fresh water trickling in to its upper reaches, and the crew of *Investigator* urgently needed water. A ship's boat was rowed up the creek as far as possible, but returned after finding 'the stream being there little better than a drain from a swamp . . . still as salt, almost, as at the ship . . .'

Geographers of the day had theorised that there was likely to be a great strait, or river, dividing New Holland (the west coast of Australia) and New South Wales. As *Investigator* made her way along the coast which no other European navigator had seen before, Flinders was buoyed by the prospect of a great geographical discovery, and the prospect 'seemed to have infused a new life and vigour into every man in the ship'.

But the morale of the whole ship, and Flinders in particular, was devastated on 23 October, when Flinders sent his trusted and able ship's sailing master John Thistle to shore at the head of the gulf (on the southernmost tip of the Eyre Peninsula) to try to find fresh water. It was a routine procedure. But on this occasion there was an inexplicable accident, the cutter they were sailing was wrecked, and Thistle and six crewmen were lost. Their bodies were never recovered. Flinders named the site Cape Catastrophe, and a large island nearby Thistle Island after his valued sailing master.

So Flinders must have felt sad and depressed as he stood on the cliff near where Ros and I had parked Penelope, and looked over a stretch of country that can only be described as desolate. Not only would he still have been grieving for John Thistle and his crew, but the miserable estuary below finally scotched any suggestion of a major waterway into inland Australia and robbed him of a significant geographical discovery.

An information board, marking the spot, quotes the entry in his diary which was as bleak as the salt flats and mangroves immediately below, and the parched desert country that stretched away to the north, east and west:

> Nothing of particular interest having presented itself to detain us at the head of the Gulf, we got under way.

Looking south towards Port Augusta, Ros and I surveyed a scene vastly different from that which greeted Flinders, but still grim—perhaps more so because of the low grey clouds that merged with the plume of smoke belching from the huge chimney of the Port Augusta power station, beyond the industrial estates and scattered buildings of the town.

Port Augusta is a good example of a town which came into being because it had to: it is a necessary conjunction of channels of communication, the point through which any traffic to the west must pass. Before road traffic, in 1851, a town was laid out, and a jetty built to service the ships which supported the pastoral leases extending into the Flinders Ranges and as far north as Leigh Creek. The port was also vital for bringing in equipment and supplies for the building of the southern section of the Overland Telegraph Line from Darwin to Port Augusta from 1871. The marginal agricultural pastures declined at the end of the nineteenth century, but Port Augusta was revived in 1912 when the Commonwealth government began building a national railway across the Nullarbor Plain to Western Australia. It is sustained to this day by the railway, power generation, and some light industry.

We did not think Port Augusta exuded any particular charm but I fear such an opinion will enrage the locals who no doubt love the place dearly. Like most travellers, we used it as a service stop and shot through as quickly as we could.

It seemed a good time to play my 'morning prayers' tape, 'Everybody's Talkin', as we were hopefully going to sunnier climes. We had plenty of unexpected rain as we headed west across the Eyre Highway. I mean, who would be a farmer? Take the wheat farmers of the Eyre Peninsula, for example. They had managed to coax a reasonable crop from their parched paddocks, despite an El Niño-induced drought. Now, in the middle of harvesting it, steady soaking rain (which they would have killed for earlier in the year) is not only reducing the quality of the grain, but the high winds are knocking it over, making it more difficult to harvest. Yet a cheerful farmer's wife in the Kimba service station was able to make jokes about it while we refuelled.

Kimba is the home of the Big Galah, looking somewhat bedraggled on that particular day, although why a district dependent on wheat production would make a feature of the destructive and voracious galah escapes me. We are heading for Wudinna about three hundred kilometres west of Port Augusta, where we plan to turn off to climb what is purported to be Australia's second-largest rock after Uluru (Ayers Rock). Weather permitting.

Penelope and The Manor are surging through the rain splendidly, although the head wind is having a disastrous effect on our fuel consumption. Penelope has 90 and 50 litre tanks, and I carry an extra 20 litres in a jerry can behind The Manor. I calculate this gives us at least 800 kilometres without refuelling. I had hoped it would be more, but towing The Manor is also burning extra diesel. I ask Ros not to calculate how many kilometres we are doing to the litre as it will only upset me.

We are now in territory first explored by Edward John Eyre in 1839. I'd been interested in finding out about Eyre, because I knew we would be following his route quite closely at times on our coastal journey to the west. Like Flinders before him, Eyre seems to have been one of those young British adventurers determined to make a name for himself in exotic parts. I had discovered that he was the son of a Yorkshire vicar and was just 17 years old when he landed at Sydney Cove on 28 March 1833 from the barque *Ellen*. His name had been put down for a commission in the Army, as various of his forebears had been soldiers. Nicholas le Eyre of Hope left one of his legs on the field of battle at Agincourt in the reign of Henry V (giving the family the dubious honour of a severed leg in armour adorning the ancestral crest). The dashing Sir Gervais Eyre lost more than a leg while defending Newark Castle for Charles I, and died in combat.

Perhaps with this in mind, Edward's clergyman father suggested the young Edward might see what he could do for himself as a settler in the new colony of New South Wales.

The tall, slim youth liked the idea, later commenting, 'I should be my own master free from all control and taking an independent [role] in life. This was the great charm.'

A courageous family background didn't provide an entree to a job, however, so when the young man failed to find clerical work in Sydney, like Charles Bonney he headed out into the countryside where he quickly gained bush skills. After working first for other settlers on the Hunter River, he was managing his own mob of sheep on his own run by his eighteenth birthday and by the time he was 21 he was such an experienced bushman and drover that he planned to drove 78 cattle and 414 sheep to the evolving settlement of Port Phillip. At this time he made contact with Captain Charles Sturt, who told him of another developing settlement in South Australia.

Eyre brought off his expedition to Port Phillip successfully. It was distinguished by his friendly approaches to Aboriginal people, already shot at by nervous European travellers who had been menaced by blacks but not actually attacked. As Eyre's party approached the Murray River on his way south, his stockmen asked for guns and ammunition to be issued to them. Eyre refused, saying that the arms were always kept in lockers outside the drays where they could be easily got at in an emergency. Later they met eight blacks, who ran after the party brandishing their spears. When Eyre stopped, so did they. The explorer dismounted, unslung his gun and laid it on the ground, making signs the Aboriginals should lay down their spears also. Then, in company with an Aboriginal companion Unmellie, Eyre greeted them in a friendly manner, smiling and handing over a knife, which was received with great delight. Such humane and tolerant dealings with Aborigines were to be the hallmark of all Eyre's exploratory journeys. Sadly, many other early English travellers and settlers were not so enlightened with their first-contact experiences.

After selling his cattle in Port Phillip, Eyre took a boat back to Sydney in October 1837. He was aware of Sturt's epic voyage down the Murray River in 1830, and that no European had yet travelled overland from New South Wales to South Australia. Sturt was planning to take stock to Adelaide himself, but generously gave him good advice on navigation and how to deal with hostile blacks. However, while Eyre was planning his expedition, he heard the unwelcome news that Joseph Hawdon and Charles Bonney were well on their way to Adelaide with a mob of cattle.

Eyre decided he would still go anyway, and set off along the Murray River. To try to beat Hawdon and Bonney, he attempted a short cut through Victoria's waterless Wimmera district and ran into terrible trouble. With five of their eight horses dead from thirst, Eyre and his companion James Baxter (who had been with him on the overland journey to Port Phillip) were forced to retrace part of their route and go north to follow Hawdon and Bonney's tracks, arriving in Adelaide in July 1838, more than three months behind Hawdon, and after nine months on the track. The Wimmera debacle cost Eyre one thousand pounds in stock losses, but he had learned a lot. 'I have acquired much practical information, knowledge and experience which may hereafter be turned to good account', he wrote.

I think it quite remarkable that despite all this hardship, he remained passionate about exploration. It was as though he saw his place in history and was determined to claim it. For one so young, he showed great maturity and courage. His father, the clergyman, who had encouraged him to go to Australia to avoid the dangers of being a soldier, might even have thought him foolhardy.

No European had travelled more than 130 kilometres north of Adelaide, and the peninsulas and their coastlines to the south were a complete mystery. On 1 May 1839 Eyre set off on his first truly exploratory expedition to try to find an adequately watered stock route to Port Lincoln. The expedition's departure was a farce. Baxter, a chronic drunk, fell off his horse into a cellar. Eyre and his three companions found water at Mt Arden near the head of Spencer Gulf and tried to push north into the same desert country that Matthew Flinders had looked towards in 1802. When he tried to head west, he was confronted with line after line of waterless sandhills. Determined to make some useful discoveries he made a sweep south-east towards the Murray where he did find some excellent grazing land.

Exploration was now a burning ambition. 'I am occupied

in interesting and important geographical researches, and have the opportunity of making my name known', he wrote to his family in England from Adelaide. A letter to a friend was even more gung-ho: 'I have gone on in the spirit of the ancient motto of our house, *Si je puis*. If I *can* distinguish myself, I *will*.'

Barely allowing Baxter enough time to sober up, Eyre sailed for Port Lincoln with unclear objectives. He was supposedly still trying to find a stock route from Spencer Gulf to Port Lincoln, but he continued 300 kilometres up the west coast of the Eyre Peninsula to Streaky Bay, then on a further 140 kilometres to Point Bell (just west of Ceduna) where he was stopped by the awesome cliffs of the Great Australian Bight and its desert hinterland. He barely made it back to Streaky Bay, then decided to head east to Mt Arden, at the head of Spencer Gulf. Probing north, he found an immense salt lake and named it Lake Torrens before turning back to Adelaide by October 1839.

There is no record that Eyre chanced upon Mt Wudinna which sprawls rather modestly across the countryside, and is 261-metres high (Ayers Rock is 335 metres). The rain had stopped when we found it and parked Penelope and The Manor at the beginning of the marked walk to the top. We decided to climb it, although walk up would be a better description. The granite rock is bordered with a low stone wall, to encourage run-off into the tanks of a nearby sheep station. The view from the top is 360° and well worth the effort, although the top-of-the-rock effect is muted by an absurd toupee of grass, scrub and stunted trees near the summit.

Onward onward along the Eyre Highway to Poochera,

where we will turn down to Streaky Bay. It is Ros's second visit to Poochera, which if you blink is unlikely to be noticed. There are the obligatory wheat silos, hotel, toilet-sized railway station, caravan park and roadhouse—not even a general store, which had burned down by the time Ros went there in 1994. But it has a heritage ant—*Nothomyrmecia macrops*. Ros made a half-hour radio documentary about it for the ABC, as part of a series on important national heritage projects, produced in association with the Australian Heritage Commission.

'How could you have made a half-hour program about an ant?'

'It's a very interesting ant', said my partner firmly.

'What does it look like?'

'I'm told it is a pale-yellow colour and has very large black eyes.'

'Do I gather that you haven't actually seen it then?'

'No.'

'You made a documentary about this unique ant at Poochera. You came here specially. But you didn't set eyes on one?'

'It is a prehistoric ant', said Ros, 'that has somehow miraculously survived in Australia. It's sometimes called the Golden Ant or the Dinosaur Ant because its closest relatives were alive when they were, 100 million years or so ago. But it only comes out of its underground nest in the dark when it's freezing cold, to climb trees to find its food. When I got to Poochera it was winter. I thought there wasn't much point in getting up at 3 am to look at an ant which wasn't going to make any noises for my tape recorder. I was, after all, making a radio program.'

Ros did interview some locals about the ant, and later

interviewed the scientist who had rediscovered it, Dr Bob Taylor, now living in Canberra. *Nothomyrmecia* had become a kind of Holy Grail for entomologists since it had first been identified. That was an unusual enough story in itself.

In December 1931, a party of amateur naturalists set out from Balladonia Station to Israelite Bay, on the south-east coast of Western Australia. The general collection of insects they found was then handed over to a remarkable woman, Amy Crocker, wife of the owner of Balladonia Station (which Ros and I planned to visit on our way west). Amy was a keen amateur naturalist and self-taught artist. She had a natural gift for drawing insects but did not, apparently, sketch either of the two specimens of *Nothomyrmecia* that had been fortunately collected. The insects gleaned on that 1931–32 expedition were sent to John Clark (a taxonomist at the Museum of Victoria) who formally described the species and gave it the full name of *Nothomyrmecia* (bastard, or false bulldog ant) *macrops* (big eyes). The discovery caused worldwide scientific excitement because the golden ant represented an early stage in evolution, when ants were evolving from wasp ancestors.

But embarrassingly the golden ant slipped off the entomological map. No one could find it again in Western Australia or anywhere else. In 1977 an American entomologist said he was coming to Australia to try to locate *Nothomyrmecia*. That dented national pride, so members of the CSIRO Division of Entomology Insect Taxonomy Group in Canberra, including Bob Taylor, decided to mount their own expedition. They headed for Western Australia, and on their way camped near Poochera about 10 pm, well short of their daily travel target. Although they were tired and frazzled from two long days' driving, they immediately began looking for insects, using helmets with battery lamps mounted on them.

It was October, it was cold, and a freezing wind was blowing in from the Southern Ocean. No one was finding anything terribly interesting and Bob Taylor decided the exercise was a dead loss. The warm caravan beckoned, with the promise of a hot drink and a good book. On his way back his headlamp shone on a couple of tree trunks which were only about ten metres from the caravan.

As Taylor later told Ros, 'I thought, "I'll just have a look there". I walked across. Immediately my lamp hit the tree it lit up a *Nothomyrmecia*. This was 1300 kilometres east of where we expected to find it, and obviously an enormous surprise.'

Taylor rushed back to the caravan, calling out the good news. (Not 'Eureka', according to a colleague, but 'the bloody bastard's here!') Another entomologist, Murray Upton, was working on a light sheet looking at some of the other insects located that night.

'He refused to believe the news until I tipped the ant out on the light sheet, and I'll never forget his eyes as he acknowledged that it was indeed *Nothomyrmecia*.' It was a dramatic first encounter with a living fossil by anyone who could identify it. Taylor said until he woke up the next morning and saw the specimens again he couldn't be sure it wasn't a dream.

It seems that *Nothomyrmecia* is a very un-antish ant. These ants don't work as a team when foraging as most ants do, nor do they divide up the major jobs, with some individuals specialising in foraging and others dedicated entirely to working inside the nest, looking after the larvae or storing food. The golden ant is an individualist, each worker sometimes labouring inside the nest, or at other times going out to forage. (The reason it only goes out on cold nights is to climb trees to sting and kill insects made torpid by the cold.)

This singular ant is not capable of leaving scent-blazed trails to guide other ants to a food source, its workers don't lick or groom their nest mates, and it has an ingenious ability to navigate its way to its food source and back to the nest by sight using the pattern of mallee branches silhouetted against the night sky like an ancient mariner's map.

Until Bob Taylor happened upon *Nothomyrmecia*, no local had ever seen it. 'If they had', said Taylor, 'they would probably have trodden on it'. The nests were found in a patch of mallee scrub, on a limestone outcrop, that had probably not been cleared for that reason.

There were further surprises. Another, bigger group of golden ants was found in a Poochera yard containing a couple of sheds which had been used by truckies overnight on their long hauls across the continent. Nearby were all kinds of discarded junk, old cable drums, rusty tins and at one stage, Taylor discovered, a small pen with pigs in it. '*Nothomyrmecia* was actually foraging on the trees, the bases of which were in the little pig pen.' The area also had tracks all through it made by young people with their trail bikes.

'Other patches of similar bush nearby yielded no *Nothomyrmecia* . We did find them in the Poochera rubbish dump. There we were, picking ants off the trees, with our headlamps glinting on broken glass and the eyes of feral cats living in the rubbish tip. So *Nothomyrmecia* tolerates pretty disturbed conditions.' There are, however, no clues to why the golden ants can't be found in other locations nearby.

There was one unfortunate setback at Poochera. Some time later Dr Bob Taylor gave directions to a Canberra colleague on how to locate the golden ants. He later got a frantic telephone call that the site was in chaos, and drove west immediately.

'It was unbelievable. Telecom had laid a phone cable through the original grove. They had come down the road verge, found a rock obstruction or some such, taken their cable under the fence, bulldozed our grove, burned the felled trees, buried the cable, and come back onto the road.' Taylor said it was as if the site had been deliberately selected for destruction! It was an accidental disturbance, but even the hardy *Nothomyrmecia* could not cope with disruption on that scale, and sadly there is now one less listed site.

Since the ants were rediscovered in the Poochera area, a further colony has been found by South Australian government entomologists about 150 kilometres to the west near Penong, but Ros told me the golden ants still haven't been found anywhere else in Australia.

The Poocherites became very excited about their 'dinosaur' ant at one point, and there was even talk of building a 'Big Ant', to match the 'Big Galah' down the road and the plethora of big oysters, big prawns, big merinos and big bananas that blight so many towns in the eastern states.

'I heard that the publican damped all that down', said Ros. 'He said he didn't think tourists would pay big money for something they couldn't see except at 3 am on cold nights.'

We are heading for the coast again, and planning to camp at Streaky Bay—also visited by Eyre—and named by Matthew Flinders in 1802. Of the many features he named along this part of the coast, it is one of the few not commemorating a member of his ship's company. Flinders thought the bands of colour in the bay must have been caused by a large river entering the ocean, but they are actually made by oils given off by the kelp. Streaky Bay had first been sighted by the Dutch explorer Pieter Nuyts in 1627—his last landfall on the southern coast of 'New Holland'. But if he named the bay, that name has not endured. Eyre established a base on the coast about three kilometres east of Streaky Bay in 1839 before beginning his epic journey to the west, across the head of the Great Australian Bight and on to King George Sound.

As has often been the case with our freewheeling progress across the continent, we have changed our minds and, although heading south-east and in a sense retracing our steps, have motored on to Venus Bay, which was NOT named by Flinders. Indeed, no one really seems to know who named it or why. One (optimistic and admittedly local) theory is that Flinders did name the bay after Venus, the Roman goddess of beauty and love. A more likely explanation is that it bears the name of the two-masted schooner *Venus* which traded around the Eyre Peninsula coastline until it was wrecked on the reef of Tumby Bay in 1850. Tumby Bay was certainly named by Flinders. So was Port Lincoln on the southern tip of the Eyre Peninsula. The coastline is dotted with reminders of Flinders' beloved Lincolnshire.

I'm becoming very fond of Matthew Flinders. It is a pity he cannot know that. Of all the early explorers, he can claim to have put his most enduring personal stamp on Australia—not only being the first to circumnavigate the continent and accurately chart so much of its coastline, but also naming it. He was the first man to consistently use the term 'Australia' when writing the account of his voyages, *A Voyage to Terra Australis*, and the name just kept on keeping on.

Like many schoolchildren who had the names and dates of the early explorers of Australia dinned into them, I'd been aware of his prominence in the exploring stakes, and found it fascinating to find out more about him. As a boy Flinders was attracted to and fascinated by the sea. He was born in Donington, Lincolnshire, in 1774. His father was a farmer, but the sea was close by and Flinders wrote in later years that he was inspired to join the navy and become an explorer when, as a schoolboy, he read Daniel Defoe's novel *Robinson Crusoe*.

Defoe is often called the father of the English novel, and *Robinson Crusoe* was the first of that genre. Certainly Defoe was an early great master of realistic narrative, drawing on the practical literary skills he honed during a long career as a journalist. His tale of a castaway on a lonely island, who had to survive on his own resources for 28 years before being rescued, was based on the real-life experience of Scottish sailor Alexander Selkirk.

Selkirk—by all accounts an exceedingly difficult character—was on a private sailing expedition in the South Seas in 1704 when he quarrelled with the ship's captain. It must have been a rip-roaring stoush because Selkirk was not marooned—he demanded the captain leave him on one of the

Juan Fernández islands, about 640 kilometres west of Valparaíso, Chile. There he cooled his heels for almost five years before being picked up by a British captain, Woodes Rogers, who wrote about how Selkirk survived in his own memoir, *A Cruising Voyage Around the World.* The teenage Matthew Flinders was captivated by *Robinson Crusoe*, which must have been heady fare with no other adventure novels in existence to compare it with at that time.

During his last year at school, Flinders wrote to his Uncle John, a sub-lieutenant, for advice on how to join the British Navy. Uncle John tried to talk him out of it, giving graphic descriptions of the hardships and loneliness of a life at sea. But he also encouraged him to study trigonometry and navigation if he was determined to join the navy. At 15, through an introduction by his sister, he met Captain (later Admiral) T S Pasley who found him a berth as a 'Lieutenant's Servant'—a way in which boys destined for the upper deck could join the service.

At the age of 16 he had the kind of lucky break that he could only have dreamed about. In 1791 he was given a midshipman's berth on HMS *Providence* commanded by Captain William Bligh, who (having survived his famous mutiny) was setting out on a second voyage to the Pacific to transport breadfruit plants from Tahiti to the West Indies. During this voyage he had his first sight of *Terra Australis* when Bligh's ship called in to Van Diemen's Land on the voyage to Tahiti. It was invaluable experience for the future explorer. On his return to England he had his only taste of naval action, in the Battle of Brest in April 1794. His patron Admiral Pasley lost a leg in the battle, and Flinders distinguished himself by showing great coolness under fire.

But he hankered to be off exploring again and, just before his twenty-first birthday, he joined HMS *Reliance* and the aptly named *Supply* on a voyage to take urgently needed food and supplies to the new settlement of New South Wales. The surgeon on *Reliance* was George Bass and on deck was a small boat, *Tom Thumb*—destined to play a major part in the exploration of the Australian coast. During the next five years when *Reliance* made a number of voyages from Britain to New South Wales with vital supplies for the new colony, both Flinders and Bass made a number of forays—sometimes together, sometimes not—exploring the virgin south-eastern coastline of the new continent. In 1798 this adventuring was rewarded by Governor Hunter, who put Flinders in command of the sloop *Norfolk* and ordered him (with Bass) to 'sail beyond Furneaux Islands, and should a strait be found, to pass through it, and return by the south of Van Diemen's Land'.

So at 24, Flinders found himself in command of his first ship, on an official voyage of discovery. The first circumnavigation of Tasmania was a triumph, and the confirmation of Bass Strait meant that passage through it would shorten the voyage from England to Sydney by at least a week.

Back in England by 1800 (Governor Hunter had sent the leaking *Reliance* back to London while it could still float), Flinders tried to find ways and means to get back to *Terra Australis* so that he could continue exploring. He wrote rather presumptuously to the distinguished botanist Sir Joseph Banks to suggest a full-scale hydrographic and scientific expedition with himself in charge. According to the historian K A Austin, author of *The*

Voyage the Investigator, this letter from a junior lieutenant to a wealthy squire was unique in British naval history. Yet Banks—the ultimate authority on *Terra Australis* at that time and an enormously influential figure in London—took up the idea. The eminent botanist must have been pleased that Flinders had diplomatically dedicated to him his publications on his Van Diemen's Land explorations.

Banks approached the Admiralty to equip the expedition. His timing was impeccable as it was known that the French government was about to send off Captain Nicolas Baudin on a similar expedition in *Le Géographe* and *Le Naturaliste*, and British prestige needed to be upheld. It was an enormous tribute to Flinders' competence as an explorer and navigator that he was entrusted with the command of *Investigator* and a major expedition at the age of 26. Flinders also knew that he had to juggle the time needed to make detailed surveys of virgin coasts with the necessity to race the French to the Antipodean prize.

The achievements of Flinders, Eyre and Bonney are extraordinary when we remember that they were all under 30.

When we reached Venus Bay a howling south-easterly was tearing across the water, with spits of rain spattering upon us. We abandoned an effort to pitch camp on the waterfront of the beautifully positioned caravan park and pushed the half-erected flapping Manor back under some sheltering trees and a steep bank in company with other more sensible campers. Two women who realised our plight helped push The Manor to the new position. Even under those conditions, Venus Bay seduced us. We felt it was time to tarry a while, after some days of consistently hard travel. But before we could lurch into a glass of red and a spag bol in the cosy comfort of The Manor, a minor disaster. On our way across the Eyre Peninsula, the driving rain had leaked into the front locker containing all my spare clothes, books, CDs, player and speakers and the Scrabble set. Clearly the roof section was not sealing down properly to the main body of The Manor—perhaps only a minor adjustment was needed, but my curses and imprecations rent the air as we wrestled with sodden clothes and wet books. Ros is always more calm and controlled in such situations (they weren't her clothes!). We will have to put everything in plastic bags in the locker until we work out why the front is letting in water.

But we are sheltered from the wind in The Manor, warm and dry, the Chateau Cardboard has been breached, and the rich smell of frying garlic and onions is promising gastronomic bliss. Our beds are dry and things could be far, far worse.

three

We Join the Grey Nomads

'Hey Ros, have a look at this, you simply won't believe it.'

I bought a copy of the Adelaide *Advertiser* from the Venus Bay Caravan Park kiosk. The front-page picture was in full colour. A beefy man in blue overalls, sunnies and a black peaked cap was caught by the camera clubbing a wounded galah—its beak agape, crest up, and one wing outstretched. The shutter had frozen the club a split second before impact. Other wounded and perhaps dead galahs littered the ground. Clearly this shot had already been despatched to newspapers around the world. It was simply amazing. So much for Kimba's Big Galah. This was a celebration of Port Lincoln's Very Dead Galahs.

And it was all official. The story, written by the *Advertiser*'s environment reporter Bronwyn Hurrell, revealed that the Port Lincoln council had authorised gun club members and other registered owners to shoot galahs at sunset when they gathered in the town's trees. As Hurrell explained, the birds create an annual nuisance in the Eyre Peninsula town when they arrive in their thousands at harvest time to feed off grain trucks arriving at the port-side wheat silos.

Not only had the pesky parrots been eating the wheat, but they were stripping the town's Norfolk Island pines, damaging television aerials and bothering the good citizens of Port Lincoln with constant squawking. So enthusiastic were the shooters that shotgun pellets had rained on to the roof of a day care centre near the railway station as children were being collected by relatives. Kane Ferguson (17) told Hurrell that he had to shield his three-year-old brother from stray pellets. Not that Kane—being a local lad with gung-ho galah attitude—was concerned about shooting them. He just thought the timing could have been better.

A motorist complained that the shotgun pellets had chipped his car's paintwork; he reported the damage to the police.

Port Lincoln's outspoken mayor, Peter Davis, wondered what all the fuss was about, particularly the plight of the preschoolers. 'Life's a risk', he said. 'Pellets raining down won't hurt you.' After all, he said, major damage was being done by the birds. 'They're worth $2000 a pair on the open market, but the only thing you're allowed to do is shoot them—and whilst I'm there it (shooting) will continue.'

I heard later that the galah shooting was stopped the following day by the State Environment Minister Dorothy Kotz after an outcry over Bronwyn Hurrell's *Advertiser* article and staff photographer Leon Mead's remarkable front-page picture. An inquiry was set up to work out a code of practice—and a less brutal way of culling the pestiferous pink-and-grey marauders than clubbing them publicly in Port Lincoln streets. A cynic might conclude that the end result was that galah culling could go on, but not in front of the tourists!

I was reminded of that infamous photograph of the South Vietnamese Police Chief General Nguyen Ngoc Loan summarily executing a Vietcong by shooting him in the head with his revolver in 1968. He was filmed as well for good measure. It might not have caused too much fuss in Saigon, but it did not play well overseas. Some say its impact in the United States media was so dramatic that it actually shortened the war.

Having decided to prop for a couple of days at Venus Bay, it was a pleasant change of routine to have a leisurely breakfast and ponder what we might do that day. The caravans around us are sheltering cheerful couples of mature years, most of whom have been slowly circulating around Australia for 12 months or more.

A television documentary, *Grey Nomads*, screened on ABC TV just before we left, is constantly in our thoughts. After all, we have joined them. Hordes of age-challenged Australians circling the continent in a variety of caravans, mobile homes, cars and camping trailers, kombis, vans and even one venerable psychiatrist on a motorcycle without sidecar. He was the ultimate minimalist camper, rejoicing when he could find something in his lightly packed saddlebags that he could throw away and do without. On the other end of the scale the program, directed and written by Steve Westh, showed a couple in a ginormous Winnebago motor home (which itself towed a covered trailer containing a four-wheel-drive vehicle) with dining room, dishwasher, washing machine, shower, toilet and queen-sized bed.

The camping rigs of other travellers are an endless source of interest to us nomads. Norm and Jean are camped nearby. They are in their mid-sixties. They have a huge caravan towed by a four-wheel drive with a 'tinny' (aluminium dinghy) strapped to the roof. Norm is a fanatical fisherman. He has circled Australia on the coastal route, Highway One, in a ceaseless quest for the ultimate fishing opportunity. They are from Fremantle, Western Australia and have been headed around Australia clockwise for nearly a year, and are almost home. The much-vaunted fishing at Lucky Bay has been a disappointment for Norm as it has been wherever he has launched his tinny and trusty outboard, all around the coast.

While he is questing at sea with rod, reel, spinners, berley and nets, Jean sits beside the caravan under the striped canvas awning and reads the latest *New Idea* magazine that she has been able to come by. She offers it to Ros, later in the day. Ros refuses it automatically, not thinking things through, and then curses herself inwardly. It would have been more diplomatic to accept. But Jean simply wanted to chat. She was looking forward to getting back to Fremantle. There were only a few weeks left now, and she was missing her grandchildren a great deal. In fact she'd been missing her house and her friends ever since she left home.

'I'm not all that keen on camping', she confided in Ros. 'But Norm just loves his fishing. Trouble is, we've been all around Australia and Norm hasn't found anywhere as good as Fremantle for fishing. He can't wait to get back now.'

Ern and Merle have been travelling with these two, on and off, ever since they met at a Queensland Gold

Coast caravan park six months ago. I have a feeling that Norm and Jean have been trying to shake them off, but I may be wrong. Grey nomad caravanners usually travel no more than 300 kilometres a day, and once they have themselves set up in a new caravan park with annexes up, TV tuned in, and new neighbours to meet, they usually stay at least a week before moving on. Norm and Jean and Ern and Merle have been doing a stately leapfrog since leaving the Gold Coast, making contact every few weeks in different caravan parks.

Norm and I had some cheerful blokey fishing talk before he roared out to sea determined to prove that he could catch more out of Fremantle than Venus Bay. Ern wasn't keen on fishing, and kept eyeing me off with a strangely puzzled expression. I knew it well. The dreaded recognition syndrome was about to come into play.

'Haven't I met you somewhere before?'

'No, I don't think so Ern.'

'I'm sure we've met somewhere. There's something very familiar about your face.'

I decided to short cut the process. 'You've probably seen me on ABC television. I used to host a program called *Backchat* for about eight years. It's probably that.'

'Ah yes—*that's* where I've seen you. Merle, I knew I'd seen Tim somewhere before, he's the bloke on the telly. We were watching you only a few weeks ago.'

'Well I stopped doing the program four years ago actually . . .'

'I'm sure we saw you. They must be repeating it.'

By this time Keith, from the third caravan down had joined the action. He and his wife had been racking their brains over my battered but faintly familiar face. He stepped over Ern's tow bar, but in his eagerness to meet me, misjudged the height, almost detaching the big toenail of his right foot on the ball-release mechanism. He was wearing thongs.

Now if I had done that, there would not only have been explosive language but a howl of anguish and despair that would have been heard in Port Lincoln, 150 kilometres south. Keith was more restrained, particularly in front of the womenfolk. 'Oh, gee', he said mildly. 'That was careless of me . . .'

I murmured my condolences and slipped away while necessary first aid was arranged. Inside The Manor Ros said crisply that she wasn't going to travel within Australia with me unless I wore a false beard and glasses. Over a cup of coffee we consulted tourist information, studied our maps and decided to run further down the coast of the Eyre Peninsula and have lunch at Elliston about 70 kilometres further south. This whole coastline is so superb we regretted not taking the coast road in the first place, instead of cutting across the top through golden ant and Wudinna Rock territory. Maybe next time.

All traces of yesterday's indifferent weather had blown away and we set off in sunshine, with that bright, washed look the countryside has after rain. Elliston has a long wooden jetty pushing out into its bay, once essential for the coastal steamers bringing in supplies to early settlers and taking away their produce. Today these jetties mostly serve as expensively maintained fishing platforms for locals and tourists, seeking tommy ruff, garfish and whiting. The visitor's attention is immediately drawn to the Elliston Hall which has a huge and startling mural on all four walls. Painted in 1992 by two local artists, Siv Grava and

John Turpie, it was completed with the help of locals and schoolchildren, and involved Aboriginal themes, fishing, early pastoral activity, transport, portraits and full-size depictions of local identities living and dead, plus sweeping land and seascapes. We followed signs to a coastal drive, and turned Penelope west on a gravel road along the top of steep limestone cliffs beside the Southern Ocean.

The road led to Blackfellows, a bluff overlooking a famous surfing break, caused by an underwater shoal about a kilometre offshore. The car park contained an eclectic collection of surfing transport, including a truck with a hut built on the tray. It was decorated with surfing murals, and carried racks of surfboards on its top. I was reminded of one of Barry Humphries' early 45 rpm records in the late 1950s called 'Chunder Down Under' when he had the surfers of the day all packed 'into the back of "Squeaky" Hudson's drinking truck', hammering up the coast 'to ride the planks'. The surfies Humphries-style had a keg in the boot 'and a few dozen tubes, and there was much chundering en route'. When the lads weren't 'zipping, cutting and flicking the boards through tunnels and wipe-outs or riding the odd bomby', they were down on the beach or in the surf club 'cracking the tubes or demolishing a twelve'.

That might have been the 1950s, but not the 1990s. The bulky wooden Malibus that weighed down Squeaky's drinking truck have given way to today's smaller sculptured, lean and mean fibreglass 'boards'. Blackfellows was clearly serious stuff. The only tubes or cans to be seen were cokes or soft drinks. Groups of surfers in wetsuits talked quietly among themselves about the conditions, clearly psyching themselves up for one of surfing's great challenges. Every now and then a surfer, wearing a light-weight crash helmet and carrying a board, trod carefully in bare feet down the narrow track among the limestone boulders that led down from the headland to the sea. Some seemed as young as 14. Looking out to sea with binoculars it was clear why the surfers were treating the occasion with respect. From time to time an enormous swell reared up literally out of the blue over the unseen reef, and rolled forward with its crest foaming. Occasionally a lone board-rider could be picked out steering precariously down the slope of this mighty wave, before turning up and disappearing into the crest with a triumphal flourish.

I realised that Ros and I were looking out into Anxious Bay, named not in honour of the mothers of the surfers risking their lives, but by Matthew Flinders in February 1802 when he found himself in this bay trapped on a dead lee shore by a fresh westerly. It seemed *Investigator* might not be able to beat her way out of trouble. Robert Brown, the expedition's naturalist, wrote in his diary that this tense situation went on for an agonisingly long time: 'all day and during the greater part of the following night we hauled our wind and were not at times without apprehension of running on shore, a catastrophe which would have terminated the voyage and probably the lives of most of us.'

A slight change of wind the next morning allowed *Investigator* to reach an anchorage behind Waldegrave Island. That was when he named the dangerous bight that had nearly trapped his ship, Anxious Bay. The point flanking the entrance to Venus Bay became Point Weyland. I thought it unlikely, in the circumstances, that Flinders had any thoughts at all of the Goddess of Love in connection with Venus Bay.

'O abandoned dunny, object d' outback art
Never to grace the smallest room or hear a …'
Nedwob

Strange stone erections in a paddock on the Eyre Peninsula—Murphy's Haystack or a giant loaf of bread?

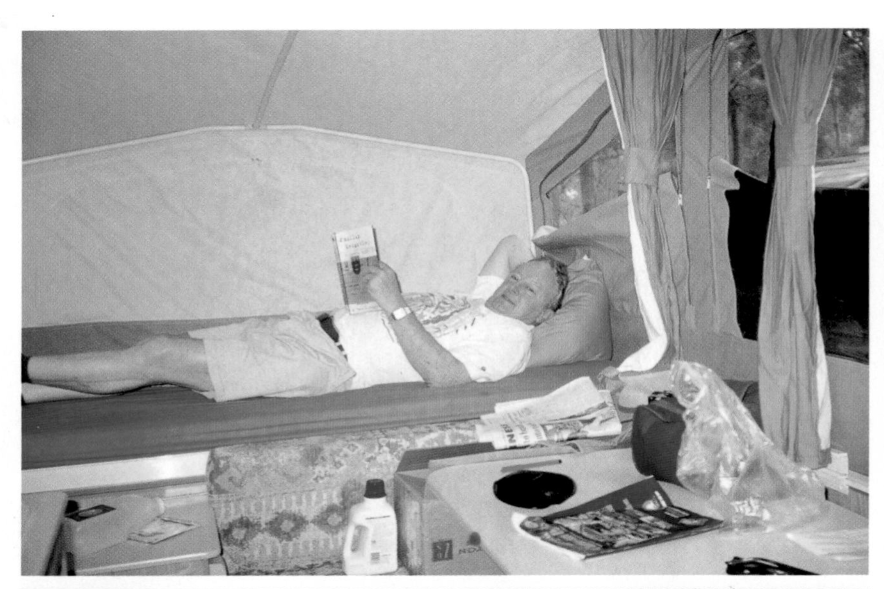

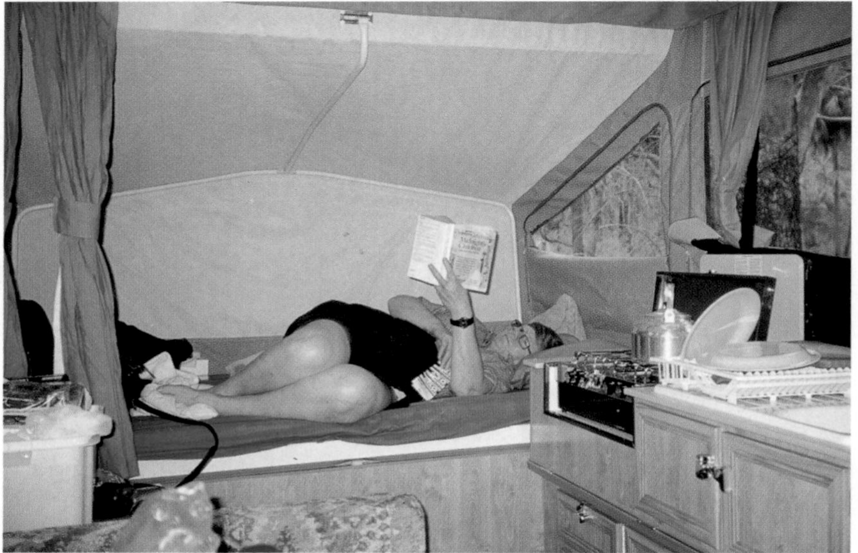

The luxury of The Manor—the trailer expands like Dr Who's Tardis.

'Nothing of particular interest having presented itself to detain us at the head of the Gulf, we got under way.' Matthew Flinders, 13 March 1802, not far from the present Port Augusta.

Clearly other travellers catch fish at Venus Bay. So why not us?

I'm a bit late. The Globe Hotel, Fowlers Bay, closed this front door for the last time in 1936—the year before I was born.

Santa comes by the mail truck at Fowlers Bay. It was a surprise for me too!

Author as Santa, with the entire student population of the Coorabie Primary School. The parental hand (right) is demanding camera attention from the moppet on Santa's knee who is more interested in her undelivered present.

The well-named Great Australian Bight. It is as though a giant cake cutter has sliced off the edge of the continent.

Somewhere out there must be a truck driver whose bull bar, sad to relate, has taken out the trifecta on the Eyre Highway—an emu, kangaroo and camel.

Two chimneys in the sifting sand are all that can be seen today of the Old Telegraph Station at Eucla which operated until 1927. Rabbits ate out the surrounding vegetation and the dunes galloped in to consume not only the Telegraph Station but the town as well.

Unkind allegations of transvestism are ignored by the fly-veiled author, seeking solace from the nostril invading Western Australian bush fly at the abandoned Deralinya Station, south of Balladonia.

Nuytsia floribunda (Christmas bush) in all its parasitic splendour. It was first seen by the Dutch explorer Pieter Nuyts in 1627 while exploring the south-west coast of Western Australia.

Balbina Station was founded in 1883 by John Paul Brooks, described rather grandiloquently as 'gentleman, pastoralist, geographer' on a bronze plaque organised by the Brooks family.

Balbina Station.
'*Here is my throne, bid kings come bow to it.*' Shakespeare

By this stage of his voyage east from King George Sound, Flinders was in virgin territory unseen by any of the early Dutch navigators. Pieter Nuyts' last landfall was Streaky Bay. Although Flinders' name is rightly associated with the first circumnavigation of Australia, his voyage along the uncharted coast of what would later be called South Australia is said to have produced greater results than any single expedition to the shores of Australia.

Despite a badly leaking ship which was also cranky and unreliable beating into the wind, Flinders accurately charted thousands of miles of the southern coastline, discovered and named hundreds of islands, and through his naturalist Robert Brown amassed one of the great botanical collections of all time. One of the driving forces behind Flinders' voyage was the growing French interest in the southern coast of New Holland. Nicolas Baudin had sailed from Le Havre with his two ships *Le Géographe* and *Le Naturaliste* in October 1800—thirteen months ahead of *Investigator*—bound for the same area. This competition was constantly on Flinders' mind, and although his British Admiralty briefing was to run east along the south coast of the continent from King George Sound in search of harbours, and to leave the detailed survey for a later visit, he was well aware that Baudin could snatch the prize of original coastal discovery from him. Flinders believed that the 'hit and run' methods of earlier explorers had prevented the detailed shape of the continent from becoming known. 'No man shall have occasion to come after me to make discoveries', was his guiding philosophy, which he put to good effect.

He took a risk in going against his instructions to do such a thorough job, but his gamble paid off. *Investigator* was at her best in the early stages of his voyage. Unfortunately for Flinders the ship's copper sheathing concealed rotting timbers. The realisation that the bottom was gradually falling out of *Investigator* made similarly detailed surveys of the Australian coast more difficult during his later circumnavigation of the continent. (Later in his circumnavigation Flinders would demonstrate the decay in his ship's timbers by poking his walking-stick through rotten patches.)

Flinders eventually did run into Baudin and his French expedition—in April, near the present Victor Harbor on the Fleurieu Peninsula, shortly after discovering and naming Kangaroo Island. It was an uneasy meeting. Unsure as to whether England and France were at war, Flinders wrote that *Investigator* 'veered around as *Le Géographe* was passing, so as to keep our broadside to her, lest the flag of truce should be a deception'. It was just as well no engagement took place, since the better-armed French could have blown the lightly gunned (and leaking) *Investigator* out of the water.

Flinders did not speak French, so took his naturalist, Brown, with him to interpret. The French crew clearly was suffering from scurvy, with characteristic pallor, listlessness and ulcerous sores. Flinders was not impressed by Baudin's account of his discoveries, even less so when the Frenchman complained about the English chart of Bass Strait, published in 1800, not realising that Flinders was one of its authors. Baudin's indecisiveness and inefficiency in getting to New Holland had enabled Flinders to beat him to an orgy of original discovery along the south coast. But Flinders made no mention of his opinion of the French explorer in his official report—apart from noting that Baudin was not happy in 'finding that we had examined the coast of New Holland thus far'.

Flinders gave the name Encounter Bay to the curve of coast where the meeting had taken place. Well, he would, wouldn't he?

Ros and I enjoyed a pleasant but basic pub lunch at Elliston before heading back to The Manor at Venus Bay. We had a plan to catch some South Australian whiting for our dinner. Neville, the cheerful caravan park manager (also a professional fisherman) had given us advice on bait, position and tide. Surely nothing could go wrong.

While we waited for the optimum fishing time, we strolled around the edge of the southern headland of Venus Bay's narrow inlet which had been hastily inspected by Flinders before he ran into pesky westerlies and tried to beat away from Anxious Bay. We had some shelter from the howling sea breeze on the windward side, and admired the kelp and the tapestry of seaweed-encrusted rock shelves just covered with crystal-clear seawater. Ros went into botanical mode and dashed about plucking bits of the local vegetation that would have to get a certificate of merit for arid land, salt resistant, survival. Every now and then we happened upon a rudimentary wooden seat, constructed by the former Labor government's Department of Employment Education and Training which provided useful projects for groups of unemployed teenagers. We appreciated the DEET seats and used all of them as we sat and contemplated the wild and beautiful sea and limestone cliffs.

Just outside the fenced-off headland reserve, in a

patch of degraded scrub between the Venus Bay houses and holiday shacks and the seaside cliff, we found intriguing small circular walls of limestone rocks protecting an odd variety of plants ranging from coastal tea-tree to improbable flowers (in that hostile environment) like gladioli and stocks. And on public land too. Then we came upon a proud, but crudely lettered sign: REG'S BOTANIC GARDEN. Reg, we later learned, was a local semi-retired fisherman with a love of gardening, a sense of humour, and a commendable sense of public-spiritedness.

We are carrying impressive beach fishing rods in a polymer tube suspended under the rear of The Manor, with state-of-the art reels. We have taken advice from Neville at the park shop. He has recommended cockles as bait, and obligingly sold us a deep-frozen pack of them. I even showed him the rig we plan to use for whiting, and received his blessing. And I also noticed there were packs of deep-frozen whiting fillets in the unlikely event we don't catch anything.

But how could we fail? If you read the local tourist literature, the waters surrounding the Eyre Peninsula and its isolated towns are full of fish fighting each other to take your bait. It is a wonder beach fishermen aren't dragged out to sea and drowned by the seething shoals of fish awaiting their offerings.

At 5 pm we walk down to the beach beside the small wooden jetty where the whiting allegedly await us. Norm, from Fremantle, is heading out into the estuary in his tinny, outboard roaring and professional-looking rods bristling in the still quite strong sea breeze. He too has taken advice from Neville. Fortunately for us the wind is off-shore and it is not hard to cast our light rigs well out into the ruffled, turquoise water. Within seconds, Ros has reeled in a small whiting which we hope is just size. South Australian fishing regulations are extremely rigorous: get sprung with an undersized fish and you can go to jail for twenty years. I believe the state fisheries authority is arguing to bring back the death penalty.

I continue to donate expensive deep-frozen cockles to the tiddlers for the next hour before landing a pathetic-looking fish, which a local lad (barely able to contain his mirth) tells me is a tommy ruff, and big enough to keep without risking a $20 000 fine.

And that was it. Norm didn't do any good either. He caught lots of undersized whiting, but threw them all back, white with fear in case a fishing inspector was accessing satellite technology to spy on him. 'I'd have a boat full of fish if I was back in Fremantle', he said wistfully.

I cleaned our two modest offerings at the fish-cleaning table. Even the three pelicans standing hopefully by looked scornful. A quick visit to Neville's freezer and a couple of rums later, we sat down to a fish dinner some of which at least had been caught by us. We had enjoyed our break at Venus Bay, but would head for Ceduna in the morning to prepare for the crossing of the Nullarbor.

Why do people in caravan parks so often come over to chat when you are either packing up, or in the act of hitching up your trailer? There are things that can go badly wrong if you don't concentrate, like not securing the safety chains, not releasing the trailer handbrake (I'd already distinguished myself by doing that) or not locking the coupling to the trailer ball.

The amiable Ern materialised from his caravan while I was wrestling with the safety chains.

'Moving on are we, Tim?'

The unworthy reply that sprang to mind was that I was doing all this for practice so I could get it right when we were *actually* leaving the next day.

'Yes Ern, time to move on.'

Caravan parks are friendly places. Norm and Jean are off this morning as well, getting a little closer all the time to good fishing at Fremantle.

As I manoeuvred The Manor slowly back to turn out of the caravan park, a sixth sense caused me to get out and double-check the trailer coupling. Just as well. Ern had distracted me. I had not locked on to the ball properly, and if I hadn't checked I would have had the camper dancing along behind me on the safety chains after the first decent bump.

It is only a modest 200 kilometres to Ceduna, and time to do some touristing. We turn off the Flinders Highway to look at Murphy's Haystacks, which are in fact unusual granite formations some of which look like haystacks. Legend has it that a coach driver told his passengers, quite seriously, that they were really haystacks. It is easy to imagine, as some of the worn knobs of granite capped with lichen stand alone and from afar seem hand-built. Like stumps of worn-down teeth the pink granite outcrops are actually connected to their jawbone—the bedrock—just below the surface of the thin soil and wisps of dry, white grass. The wind has shaped some of these exposed rocks into wonderful Rodin-like sculptures.

It is a place that encourages quiet contemplation and an awareness of the aeons of time that have worn down the first jagged profiles of the Australian continent. The land is privately owned, and the Cash family (descendants of the haystacks' Mr Murphy) encourage visitors. There are a picnic table and dunny at the gate, and an honesty box for a modest donation to maintenance costs. We found it a delightful diversion, only two kilometres from the Flinders Highway.

With such a comparatively short distance to Ceduna, we decided to run down to the coast and lunch at Smoky Bay—a small settlement distinguished by the phallic finger of its huge wooden jetty poking out into the bay, and its superb local oysters which we demolished under a Norfolk Island pine on the seafront. Flinders named the bay after the plumes of smoke he saw from *Investigator*—probably from Aboriginal fires. For some reason this bay, and its off-shore islands, received a great deal of attention from early explorers.

The islands of St Peter and St Francis were named by the Dutch navigator Pieter Nuyts in 1627. No written reports of Nuyts' voyage survive to tell us what he thought of the lands he had seen on the southern coast of New Holland, but they must have been fairly favourable, because an employee of the Dutch East India Company, one Jean Pierre Purry, put forward an ambitious scheme in 1717 for the Dutch to colonise the area. He argued that the Land of Nuyts would have an ideal climate because of its latitude. He compared its position in the world with California, Florida, Chile and the Cape of Good Hope and postulated that the Land of Nuyts would bring the company immense profits, which could be anticipated 'with inconceivable joy' in 'cheese, wine, olives, tobacco, or chief of all silkworms'.

Perhaps fortunately for Purry's future with the East India Company his hyperbole was ignored. He had a fertile imagination because his proposal also canvassed the possibility that there may have been giants in the Land of Nuyts, 'not only in stature, but even in intelligence and knowledge, so prodigious that their likes have never been seen or heard of in any other country in the world'. How or why he put this forward is unknown. Perhaps he was smoking some 'wacky baccy' while working on his report. But in 1718 he published his ideas in a small booklet believed to have influenced Jonathan Swift, beginning work at that time on his celebrated *Gulliver's Travels*.

Swift has Lemuel Gulliver 'driven by a storm to the north-west of Van Diemen's Land', and shipwrecked at 30° Latitude. The only known islands near there were St Francis and St Peter, and could have well been the model for Lilliput. But instead of Purry's giants, Swift opted for midgets.

Early explorers along this coast had buzzed around the islands like busy blowflies. Flinders, when he got to Streaky Bay, realised he hadn't seen much of the coast since leaving the islands of Nuyts Archipelago, so he sailed back and poked about mapping the islands and searching for non-existent freshwater rivers. His French rival Baudin got as far as the Nuyts Archipelago after his meeting with Flinders at Encounter Bay in April 1802. But four weeks later his crew were so sick with dysentery and scurvy that he temporarily abandoned his survey and took off for Port Jackson in New South Wales 'for truly we were all very much in need of a little rest'. But he was back in February the following year with *Le Géographe* and a replacement ship for *Le Naturaliste*, *Le Casuarina*, bestowing French place names with great diligence. As Flinders had done a pretty thorough job along that coast just before him, few have stuck. But he did well around Ceduna. There is Murat Bay, named after one of Napoleon's marshals, and among other Gallic discoveries are Cape Thevenard, Masillon Island, Decres Bay and Cape D'Estress.

Driving towards Ceduna you wonder how the early pastoralists ever thought they could win a living from such a parched, desiccated landscape. We are conscious of leaving the small outposts of human activity that dot the Eyre Peninsula and heading into an arid void. Ceduna is the last major settlement before tackling the Nullarbor Plain, shorthand for the 1300 or so kilometres of mallee-scrub wilderness between Ceduna in South Australia, and Norseman in Western Australia—the first town of any size other than remote refuelling points to be reached after leaving Ceduna. Our sense of adventure and anticipation is growing—not that we are likely to perish in the desert, but all the written and spoken advice emphasises the importance of ensuring your vehicles are in sound mechanical condition, because there are only rudimentary repair possibilities along that section of the Eyre Highway. It would be an expensive tow, or freight job, to rescue your car or caravan from an outpost like Cocklebiddy. We have a good, reliable rig, but there is always the unexpected.

Ceduna's deep-water port (with familiar grain silos) is on

the promontory of Thevenard, with Murat Bay on the western side, and Bosanquet Bay to the east. Ceduna was surveyed first in 1896, and was proclaimed a town five years later. Its name is appropriate—from the Aboriginal word 'chedoona' meaning 'a resting place'. Most transcontinental travellers do just that before attempting the Nullarbor.

The waterfront caravan park at Ceduna is admirable, with a sensible layout for caravans, trailers and tents, plenty of shade trees, efficient and clean toilet blocks (always a benchmark for traveller satisfaction) and Vicki at the kiosk a veritable fount of useful information, not only about Ceduna, but the crossing of the Nullarbor. She has prepared her own mud map for her customers, with the cheapest fuel stops marked, and even recommendations about which of the five lookout points along the great cliffs of the Great Australian Bight to visit if you haven't time for them all. Vicki also tells us that the fruit and veggie inspection on the Western Australian border is merciless. Even onions and garlic are *verboten* and she had doubts too about a packet of sun-dried tomatoes. While sympathetic to the Sandgropers' determination to be free of evil eastern states plant diseases, for us there is a practical problem. Most travellers restock their fruit and veggies at Norseman, but we are planning to turn down to the south coast at Balladonia, about 200 kilometres before Norseman, and explore the country east of Esperance. Looks like no taties, onions, or fresh greens for at least a week.

We have the afternoon free for some local exploration, and turn Penelope's nose towards Denial Bay, named by Matthew Flinders of course! But this bay has to rank as one of his more obscure nomenclature efforts. For once it was not named after a member of his ship's company, physical happenings like smoky fires, human catastrophe, or perhaps an 'encounter' with wandering French persons. (Nicolas Baudin, like Flinders, had high hopes of finding the expected inlet to a major river, or gulf, opening up the interior among the many bays and headlands on this part of the coast.)

So the bay sheltered by the island of St Peter became Denial Bay, 'as well in allusion to St Peter as to the deceptive hope we had found of penetrating by it some distance into the interior country'. Flinders doubtless had in mind St Peter's three denials of Christ just before the crucifixion. The bay certainly denied them useful access into the continent. As did every other inlet along the entire southern coast of Australia.

We are in William McKenzie country, McKenzie being an engaging pioneer who was allotted a block of 17 800 acres in 1889, and who built a homestead about three kilometres west of the present township at Denial Bay. He was also close enough to the landing point in the bay—known as McKenzie's Landing—to be helpful to the hopeful wheat and sheep farmers and their families flocking to the new blocks opened up in the 1890s. 'Mac' met them with his five-horse team to haul their goods ashore at low tide, and then acted as a kind of unofficial host and mentor. His homestead developed through the last decade of the nineteenth century into what was essentially a small town with several cottages, a blacksmith's shop, post office, saddlery, slaughter house and his own large home with a dining room which could seat fifty guests. 'Mac's Town' as it was called, became the social hub of the district for ten years, until the Denial Bay township took over. McKenzie became a Justice of the Peace, and gave jobs to many a new settler until he became established.

There's not much left of Mac's Town these days but a few crumbling brick walls and the large stone-and-concrete-lined underground tanks for precious and scarce drinking water. Some of the settlers were forced to cart sea water from the ocean and condense it into fresh water by boiling it in cauldrons with wood fires—a laborious, inefficient, but vital process.

There's a stone memorial to William McKenzie at the remains of Mac's Town. He was born in Adelaide in 1844 and died in 1906. His profound contribution to the philosophy of arid-land farming is inscribed on a small bronze plaque: 'You can't grow wheat with your hands in your pockets.' Good one, Mac.

These days Ceduna not only ships out grain, but the deep-sea port at Thevenard also bulk handles gypsum and salt and is the second most profitable port in South Australia. There's a big fishing industry there and two fish-processing factories. We went to one, lured by the prospect of cheap seafood. Unfortunately they would only sell it to us in frozen five-kilo packs, and The Manor's tiny fridge could not cope. We managed to get some fresh fillets of prized King George whiting at the local fish shop, and returned to the caravan park in good spirits. Norm and Jean (the Fremantle couple we met at Venus Bay) are camped nearby. Norm had been out fishing but hadn't done much good. I was surprised to hear that 'had I been back at Fremantle it would have been a different story'. I said, 'Norm—you can't catch fish with your hands in your pockets'. He looked puzzled.

A circumferentially challenged family is camped just behind us. The husband and wife and two teenaged children are amazingly overweight. The husband, who is steadily and impressively drinking his way through a whole carton of cold beer, bears an uncanny resemblance to Onslow in the British television series *Keeping Up Appearances*. Onslow is the slobby brother-in-law of the socially pretentious Hyacinth Bucket (pronounced Boo-quay as she incessantly reminds us) played by actress Patricia Routledge. The television Onslow is a physical catastrophe, with permanent stubble, gross beer belly, baseball cap, and a predilection for being a couch potato in front of the telly with a large can of beer clutched in one beefy hand and a bag of crisps in the other. 'Onslow' and I greet each other cheerily on our respective treks to the used beer department. I wonder if he has ever watched the series?

We have one more pilgrimage before heading across the Nullarbor. Fowlers Bay, some 150 kilometres west of Ceduna, is where Edward John Eyre made his base camp before deciding to attempt his epic journey around the Great Australian Bight to Western Australia. And, yes, it too was named by Flinders, after his first lieutenant, Robert Fowler. It was also the centre of one of the earliest pastoral settlements in the far west of South Australia, where William Swan established his Yalata Station in 1860. How or why he thought he could run sheep, cattle or grow grain on this impoverished country seems beyond imagination, but perhaps the land was less degraded then. The far west (as the South Australians refer to the area) still does support a modest pastoral industry of grain, wool and cattle, but the bypassing of Yalata (Fowlers Bay) by the

Eyre Highway in the 1940s signed the death warrant of what had been a sizeable town. Just how big we were about to find out.

There is a good gravel road down to Fowlers Bay and by midmorning we turned into the fairly basic caravan park and camping area, surrounded by a sheet-metal windbreak. The only other occupants were just leaving. Ken and Liz were South Australian farmers, and had decided to take a break on the road. Ken's Nissan four-wheel-drive utility looked businesslike, with extra winch cable wound around the front bull bar, and a small cab built behind the cabin. I noticed a stainless-steel beer keg was slung under the rear of the tray—almost certainly for extra water rather than the amber fluid, although Ken is one of those Australians who seems to have a cold can in a stubby-holder permanently welded into his right hand. Ken looked as durable as his vehicle, with ample belly, a splendidly sweat-stained, battered Akubra with ventilation holes worn through the crown, and hands and forearms like a navvy. He looked as tough as the proverbial mallee root. However, I thought his greeting a little strange.

'Welcome to Fowlers Bay, Santa Claus. Would you like some bait?'

By 11 am it was already around 30° Celsius and the tired-looking squid, prawns and cockles were widely advertising their demise in the warming water at the bottom of his bait bucket. But it seemed churlish to refuse. We could see the customary big jetty jutting out into the bay opposite the camping ground, and we had already heard glowing reports of all the fish to be had at Fowlers Bay. But why is it that whenever we get to a good fishing spot the wind is up, and the tide wrong? I put the bait in the shade of the sheet-metal windbreak, which was the best I could do at that stage.

'What's this Santa business?'

'You'll find out. Which way are you heading?'

'Across to the west.'

'So are we. I'll keep a lookout for you.' Ken gunned the motor of the Nissan as he began to tow their caravan out of the rather stark compound. 'Then I can find out how you got on with the kids . . .'

A cheery wave from Liz and they were gone.

Christmas was still a week away. Ros and I walked along the waterfront to the store with one petrol pump that also doubled as the caravan park office—and just about everything else in Fowlers Bay. Morrie and Marg were waiting to pounce.

'Thank Gawd—here's Santa at last', boomed Morrie. 'That other bloke was going to do it, but he shot through. So now you're it.'

I thought Ken had seemed in a hurry. There didn't appear to be any choice in the matter. It turned out that the Coorabie Primary School was having its end-of-term picnic, and that a visit from Santa was the highlight.

'The only trouble is', said Morrie, 'all the kids know me by now. I've done it so many times before. That's why we need you.'

There was time for some fishing from the jetty before I became Mr Ho Ho Ho. In any case, I had to wait for the mail truck to arrive—the far west substitute for reindeers and a sleigh. The sea breeze was well and truly in, which didn't do much for the fishing but at least it blew the smell of Ken's ripening bait well away. We tried fishing from the jetty, just off the beach, with no luck, so we made the long trek to the end of the jetty where Ros caught a reasonably sized leatherjacket on her first cast. I was struggling with wind, weed and pessimism. Conditions didn't get any better and the wind got so strong it blew the bucket over, spilling the bait on the planks of the jetty—which was a mixed blessing. We gave it away after an hour, and walked back along the jetty to find a small cluster of locals using the very spot, and sand patch, that we had tried first. They were hooking portion-size trevally out of the water with commendable expertise. It must be the way they hold their mouths. The locals I mean.

Morrie was waiting for me at the caravan park with a suitcase. 'Here's the Santa gear, mate. Barry, the mailman, is running a bit late, but I've got a message to him to call in here to pick you up, before he goes around to the community centre. You'd better get changed, he could be here any moment. The kids are all down at the beach having a swim. We'll bring them up to the hall as soon as we see the mail truck.'

The Santa kit was impressive, and provided by the Coorabie Primary School. Apart from the red suit (with big safety pin thoughtfully provided for girth adjustment), there was a long white wig, an impressive beard with moustache attached, and black cloth leggings to simulate boots. A striped pillowslip fleshed out with some empty cardboard boxes completed my ensemble. The Manor provided a little shade, and I stood there waiting for Barry, sweating in full fancy dress except for the red, fur-trimmed Santa hat which I figured could wait until the last moment. Still, I presented a fairly bizarre sight, and the next two campers to drive in to the park clearly thought so too. It could have been one of them, I brooded . . .

Half-an-hour later Barry clattered in the gate with his truck, and Morrie materialised with balloons and streamers to tie on the cab. Horn blaring, Santa arrived, with much ho-hoing and excitement. I could see some of the older kids eyeing me off trying to see who I was, but the disguise was perfect. Anyway, there was Morrie in his blue singlet and shorts as large as life among the crowd.

I babbled some nonsense about having broken a runner of the sleigh near Penong on the Eyre Highway and having to hitch a ride with Barry on the mail truck, leaving Dancer and Prancer and Donner and Blitzen and the rest of the reindeers happily eating wheat stubble in a paddock with some sheep.

In the old days Coorabie was a one-teacher school, with all the children catered for in the one classroom. These days there are two teachers, and Santa's flock of about 15 kids ran from preschool dribbling toddlers to a startlingly tall, bright-eyed Aboriginal girl of about eleven. All sat on Santa's knee in their wet bathing suits while I did my best with presents and small talk. I was able to get by with one-day cricket comments with some of the older boys, but had to fall back on ho-hoing and 'what do you want for Christmas' for the sprogs. With a flash of inspiration I got them all singing 'Jingle Bells', and then ran out of puff. I made a break for the mail truck and got in, but there was no Barry! It was the most protracted goodbye since Melba. I ho-hoed away and waved for what seemed an eternity before Barry materialised from the shop, kicked his old truck into gear, and delivered a very hot and frazzled Santa with salty damp trousers back to The Manor.

During the cool of the evening we strolled around the remains of what had once been a flourishing town. It was an important repeater station for the Overland Telegraph line to Western Australia, and the telegraph station was built in 1876, with the long stretch to Eucla completed the following year.

Some of Yalata's historic buildings still exist, including the telegraph office, Institute Hall, police station and courthouse, and harbour master's house. The remains of the Globe Hotel are a sad sight, almost completely covered by the sand dunes which have crept up on the town. The rather splendid front door is still there, with its massive stonework a guide to past glories. We were a bit late for a drink. Convivial home to generations of farmers, transcontinental travellers and kangaroo shooters since 1897, it closed its doors for the last time in 1936 after a rip-roaring last day. The publican, Reg Betts, had turned on free drinks. A contemporary account described how one Ellis Cabot 'was swinging from the gaslights like the Man on the Flying Trapeze'. In the midst of the celebrations Betts then auctioned off all the stock and furniture.

As Ceduna grew, Fowlers Bay declined. The tyranny of distance delivered the coup de grace, when Yalata failed to get a rail spur from Penong, and the main highway to the west was constructed further north.

That evening Ros stretched her leatherjacket by currying it (I refer to the fish—we weren't that short of rations) and adding all the vegetables we would otherwise have to sacrifice at the Western Australian border. I went to sleep dreaming vividly of Edward John Eyre, thirsty and stumbling through the saltbush and sand dunes. It was a windy night. The curry was to blame, without question.

four

When Can I Buy Another Tomato?

We woke seized by a manic determination to catch some fish. Were we not in a beach-fishing paradise? The wind has swung around to the south-west—offshore at Fowlers Bay, but not good news for Scotts Beach where we had planned to fish. Morrie, the genial mine host of the caravan park, suggested we went further west along the coast to Mexicans Hat Beach which would be more sheltered. Salmon and flathead, he assured us, were waiting to commit suicide on our hooks.

Penelope seemed to relish the deeply trenched sand tracks running behind the coastal dunes, so we didn't need to engage four-wheel drive. Mexicans Hat Beach was a doddle to identify because of a pinnacle of rock, rising from a circular formation looking, well . . . like a Mexican's hat. With rods at the ready we picked our way down the small limestone cliff to the pristine beach and startlingly clear water. The cliff did offer some shelter, but the south-westerly was so strong that it funnelled around the point, sandblasting our legs, and made casting out not only difficult but wellnigh impossible. Still, one of the things they do say about beach fishing is that it is an excuse to get to nice places. We tried Morrie's expensive deep-frozen pilchards on ganged hooks for salmon, cockles for whiting, and prawns for any bloody thing that might be about.

Before we left for the west, I told my 91-year-old father that we had high hopes of beach fishing on the way. He expressed incredulity from his native Tasmania. 'Have you ever seen anyone beach fishing catch a fish?' I had to admit that I hadn't. 'Neither have I', he said. 'I've often wondered why people do it. It can't have anything to do with actually catching fish.' (Tasmanians believe that there is no point going fishing if you don't come home with a feed for the whole family and the neighbours as well.)

Before buying our expensive rods and reels, however, Ros and I had observed other beach fisherpersons on the New South Wales coast—few women seem to beach fish—and noted the expressions of Zen-like contentment on their faces while envying their inner peace.

I felt it would be even more spiritually satisfying if we actually caught some fish. Ros, a redhead, had forgotten her suncream and noticed her legs were turning crayfish-red. The wind was getting stronger, and our karma was fraying around the edges. On the way back to camp we stopped to photograph the crumbling stone ruins of a shepherd's cottage, and drove to a headland to look along windswept Scotts Beach. It was near here that Eyre and his party camped for many weeks at an Aboriginal water-soak in the dunes before he committed himself to the huge coastal trek around the head of the Bight to Albany.

After his exploratory journeys on the Eyre Peninsula in

1839, Eyre decided to take a shipload of sheep to Albany. In Perth he met Lieutenant John Lort Stokes, second in command of HMS *Beagle*, who reported the discovery of two great rivers leading southward: the Adelaide River on the north coast and the huge Victoria River on the far north-west coast. Stokes told Eyre that the headwaters of these rivers might be deep in central Australia—perhaps draining the much sought-after inland sea.

Back in Adelaide Eyre told South Australia's Governor Gawler that more exciting possibilities lay north beyond the Flinders Ranges rather than trying to open a stock route to Western Australia, and offered to lead such an expedition and finance a third of its costs. (He finished up having to pay half of it.) Two days after Eyre dined with the governor, Charles Sturt threw his support behind the idea at a public meeting on 29 May, and later that day Gawler summoned Eyre and told him he would command that expedition. Eyre was 23.

The expedition set off on 18 June 1840 and included the faithful Baxter, four other Europeans and two of the Aboriginal boys who had travelled with Eyre before. Cootachah, about 11, had been with him since 1837 and Neramberein—a few years older—since 1839. Although they were so young, and a long way from their Murray-Murrumbidgee homelands, their bush skills were invaluable. Eyre referred to them as 'Yarry' and 'Joey' in his journals, and was fond of them in a fatherly kind of way. They often slept in his tent.

(I was fascinated to discover that they were so young because in April the following year they were to shoot Baxter in Western Australia, when Eyre's by then much smaller party had almost succeeded in reaching the western side of the Great Australian Bight. Lacking the life-experience of older men, youthful panic probably played a big part in this useless and tragic killing—but I am jumping ahead.)

Curiously he did not include Wylie, an Aboriginal he had brought back with him from his voyage to King George Sound in Western Australia. Perhaps the prospect of a western journey at some time in the future was in his mind.

We will not be attempting to follow Eyre's northern journey with Penelope and The Manor on this particular odyssey (although we'll keep it in mind for another time) so I'll not dwell on Eyre's three-month saga attempting to push north into central Australia—foiled by the great saltpans of Lake Torrens and Lake Eyre which he mistakenly believed were one and the same.

Having been unable to penetrate north into central Australia, he made his way to his old stamping ground, the Baxter Hills (near Iron Knob on the Eyre Peninsula), and sent Baxter west towards Streaky Bay with the main party while he went south to the settlement of Port Lincoln to get urgently needed supplies. For most of his way he followed the wheel ruts of his wagons, still clearly evident from his southern journey in 1839—something four-wheel drivers of today might ponder as they scrub-bash into virgin territory over our fragile desert lands.

Eyre sent one of his men to Adelaide by sea with his despatches, charts and geological specimens. He managed to replace one of his lost horses with a Timor pony, and buy twelve sheep and a small boat to help with coastal exploration of the fabled inland sea.

Then he linked up with the rest of his party, who were in good shape, gorging themselves with oysters from Streaky Bay. He sent his little cutter *Waterwitch* on to Fowlers Bay, where he already knew water could be found. The party reached Fowlers Bay without losing any sheep or horses because Eyre (unlike less-aware explorers such as Burke and Wills, who perished in country where Aboriginal people flourished) asked the advice of local Aborigines who showed him where wells could be dug among the sand dunes.

Eyre was fascinated by the way blacks lived off the land, 'procuring their food as they went along, which consisted of snakes, lizards, goannas, bandicoots, rats, wallabies etc. It was surprising to see the apparent ease with which, in merely walking across the country, they procured an abundant supply for the day.'

I still find it difficult to believe that Burke and Wills weren't more curious about how the Aborigines all around them were finding food and water, while they were perishing from hunger and thirst. Mind you, even twentieth century British explorers could be dogmatic and impervious to common sense about their methods. What about that prize dunderhead Robert Falcon Scott in the Antarctic? Among his other planning disasters for his South Pole venture, Scott eschewed the use of husky dogs to pull the expedition's sledges for 'the martyrdom of man-hauling, to which in a spirit of self-mortification, official British explorers had become addicted'.

Without Aboriginal help, Eyre would never have made it across the continent—a reality he freely acknowledged in his journals. Ever open-minded (and no doubt conscious of the dangers of scurvy), his party ate the same red berries the Aborigines were gathering during this part of the journey. The Europeans turned on a feast of rice, tea, salt beef and damper as a reward for all the guidance and help these original Australians had given them.

I can't say that Ros and I were doing well living off the land—or I should say sea. My venerable father seemed to be right about beach fishing. It is something people do to justify being in a nice environment, but has little to do with catching fish. As if to prove his point, two young men have just come into the Fowlers Bay caravan park with four-wheel drive, bristling with fishing rods mounted on specially constructed racks on the bullbar, their vehicle bulging with eskies and a portable fridge. Surely they must have scored some fish? Well, as it happened—no. They told us they had actually been casting into shoals of salmon which had completely ignored their expensive lures and fresh bait. They had caught one clumsy fish which did not take their bait, but accidentally jagged itself on to one of their hooks.

Fowlers Bay has a particularly splendid wooden jetty, projecting at least a kilometre out into the bay. Such jetties are as much a feature of coastal towns on the Eyre Peninsula as are the concrete wheat silos marking the small settlements inland. We heard on ABC news that the South Australian government is trying to hand over maintenance of these jetties to the local councils, a cost of about $130 000 for each jetty—working out, due to the area's sparse population, at an annual impost of about $1200 per head! Not surprisingly the councils were crying foul.

We are pleased we decided to spend two nights here before tackling the Nullarbor. Eyre was here for much longer. It was summer and hot—the worst time for attempting travel in waterless country. By then he had made up his mind to press west, no matter what, so while he was waiting for *Waterwitch* to return, he tried again to reach the head of the Bight with two companions, carrying as much water as he could on horseback. It was a frightful struggle against heat and thirst, and again he could not have survived had he not been led to soakage wells by friendly blacks. The most important discovery of this six-week ordeal was to discover a native well, known as Yeerkumban-kauwe, at the head of the Bight. But the Aborigines had also made it clear to Eyre that there was no water further west on top of the great rocky cliffs that seemed to stretch to eternity around the Bight.

In January 1841 a sail was sighted from Fowlers Bay. It was not *Waterwitch*, which had sprung a leak, but another vessel, *Hero*. On board was Wylie, the Aboriginal Eyre had recruited from King George Sound in Western Australia and who would be invaluable on the trek west. Eyre decided the journey was too risky to take any other Europeans save the trusty Baxter who was totally committed to Eyre and the journey, plus the two younger Aboriginal boys Neramberein and Cootachah as well as Wylie. He sent the rest of his party back to Adelaide on *Hero*.

On 23 February, just as they were burying extra stores before leaving, they heard shots from Fowlers Bay. To their surprise they met with the captain of *Hero* and Edward Scott (whom Eyre had just sent back to Adelaide). There were letters and despatches imploring Eyre not to attempt the unknown 1500 kilometre overland trek to Albany. But Eyre was single-minded about his westward journey. He made starkly clear to the unwavering Baxter his '. . . firm determination never to return unsuccessful, but either to accomplish the object I had in view, or perish in the attempt'.

At the end of February 1841—the hottest time of the year—Eyre, his four companions, ten horses, a Timor pony and six ration sheep headed west through the coastal sand dunes literally to do or die.

Ros and I were setting off from Fowlers Bay in December with less dramatic alternatives—although I was deeply concerned whether Ros had allowed enough space for life-sustaining cold beer in Penelope's small onboard refrigerator. Ros had also revealed on the morning of our Nullarbor Plain run that her careful planning had not included parmesan cheese for our next spaghetti bolognaise. With no vegetables obtainable for the foreseeable future, this was a serious blow to our gastronomic prospects. Our only hope was the Aboriginal-run Yalata Roadhouse, the next service stop before the Western Australian border. I did not have great expectations of being able to pick up any parmesan cheese there.

The weather was so cool we did not need airconditioning as we headed north-west to rejoin the Eyre Highway after the diversion to Fowlers Bay. A couple of weeks ago it was 44° Celsius at Ceduna! We passed the Coorabie Primary School, whose teachers never knew the identity of the travelling 'multi-mediocre-personality' who did his best to entertain their students from the anonymity of the school's Santa suit.

Although it is early on a Sunday morning it seems to be peak hour for road trains and semitrailers on the Eyre Highway, mostly heading east. They roar past, their slipstream rocking Penelope and The Manor. We are running out of fenced country, having left most of the wheat paddocks behind us, although the South Australian far west wheat belt extends well to the north-west of nearby Yalata Station. One of the reasons I try never to travel at night in outback Australia is the danger of hitting kangaroos. The road trains just plough on through the night, and the Eyre Highway is littered with dead 'roos as a result—at times one every 400 metres or so. Whether this nightly slaughter supports an extra population of wedge-tailed eagles I know not, but these huge birds have developed a remarkable tolerance for traffic. They flap lazily away at the last second when they are feeding on a carcass in the middle of the road. Those at the roadside do not even disengage their talons as they tear and stab at the rotting flesh, with cars and trucks howling past only a metre or so from them.

We had heard all kinds of horror stories on the road about alcohol-generated scenes of squalor and violence surrounding the Aboriginal-managed Yalata Roadhouse. I must say it was pretty quiet at 11 on a Sunday morning and I have nothing but fond memories of it. Not only did the shop come up trumps with a *Weekend Australian* newspaper complete with its colour magazine and feature sections, but some parmesan cheese! An obliging counter attendant 'borrowed' some for us from the restaurant kitchen. Are there to be no travel deprivations?

The vegetation is thinning as we get closer to the Nullarbor Plain, which is a misnomer. Alfred Delisser, the first explorer to make a significant journey inland through the region in 1866, named it after the Latin *nulla* (no) *arbor* (tree). Yet the three million hectares of the Yalata Aboriginal Lands from the Eyre Peninsula across to

Western Australia are largely covered with the durable mallee eucalypts, as well as saltbush, bluebush and other desert plants. This is limestone country, the bed of the inland sea that all those early explorers from Flinders to Eyre were looking for. But they were 100 million years too late.

Not only that, by the time Flinders and Eyre came on the scene the seabed had been lifted up to form a great level plain, bordered on the seaward side by the spectacular limestone cliffs of the Great Australian Bight. This region is so featureless that the Trans-Australian Railway boasts the longest completely straight stretch of track in the world—479 kilometres.

After we passed the turn-off to the Head of the Bight (a popular vantage point to see migrating southern right whales from June to October) the Eyre Highway ran down to within sight of the Southern Ocean, and only a few hundred metres from the cliff edge. We've all seen the photographs, but they do not prepare you for the reality of those limestone ramparts standing against the great swells rolling in unhindered from Antarctica, smashing against the base of the cliffs in a welter of foam and white water. It is as though a giant biscuit-cutter cutter had trimmed off the edge of the continent.

Matthew Flinders was not the first navigator to sight the cliffs of the Great Australian Bight, but he was the first to try to chart them. As he sailed east along the coast in 1802 he was looking at the great limestone edge of the Nullarbor Plain, which continues unbroken for more than 800 kilometres. On 19 January he lamented in his log:

> A surveyor finds almost no object here whose bearing can be set a second time. Each small projection presents the appearance of a

> steep cape, as it opens out in sailing along; but before the ship arrives abreast of it, it is lost in the general uniformity of the coast . . .

By 27 January he had reached the head of what he called in his log 'the great bight or gulph of New Holland', and twelve years later when writing *A Voyage to Terra Australis* gave it the name we know it by today.

As he worked his way along the southern coast of *Terra Australis* he was puzzling over the solution of another navigational problem for which countless generations of later seafarers would thank him.

Anyone who visits a ship's bridge to this day will notice that the magnetic compass is located between two spheres of soft iron. A cylindrical bar of metal runs along in front of the compass and is known as 'Flinders' Bar'.

Flinders knew, as did the seafarers of earlier centuries, that the earth's magnetic field is not constant, and that compasses vary accordingly in relation to your position on the earth's surface. This had been noted, through the years, by observation so that variations were allowed for by navigators as they moved around the globe.

Enough was known about magnetism to ensure that the ship's compass was isolated in a binnacle—a stand of non-magnetic metal, usually brass—to protect it from the influence of ferrous metals. A helmsman knew that even a knife carried on his belt would affect the compass.

What was not known at the beginning of the nineteenth century was that each ship has its own magnetism which exerts an extra influence on the compass.

Like all good navigators, Flinders wanted his charts to be as accurate as possible. Yet he noticed, with frustration, that his compass bearings varied considerably each time his ship changed course. On 17 February, while beating past a dangerous lee shore at Avoid Bay (shortly before sailing up Spencer Gulf for yet another inland-sea disappointment), he conducted some experiments by removing two carronades from the quarter-deck near the binnacle, as he suspected that their iron affected the compass. He wrote later in *A Voyage to Terra Australis*:

> Differences like this of 5½°, which frequently occurred, seemed to make accuracy in my survey unattainable, from not knowing what variation to allow on the several bearings. The guns were removed in the hope to do away the differences, but they still continued to exist, nearly in the same proportions as before; and, almost in despair, I at length set about a close examination of all the circumstances connected with them, in order to ascertain the cause, and if possible to apply a remedy; but it was long, and not without an accumulation of facts, before I could arrive at the conclusions deduced . . .

Flinders' breakthrough was to discover the principle of deviation—that the movement of a ship through 360° caused the compass to vary predictably at various points. This led to the practice of 'swinging the compass', where a ship was taken to a special location, and swung around 360°, stopping every 10° to take a bearing on a fixed point, and then calculating the magnetic deviation generated by the ship. So what is known as a *true* course today is arrived at by adding the *variation* caused by the earth's magnetic field, and the *deviation* (courtesy of Matthew Flinders) caused by the ship's own magnetic field, and subtracting both from the magnetic compass bearing.

There are five lookouts where you can drive to a car park and walk 100 metres or so to vantage points looking along the limestone cliffs of the Great Australian Bight. Remembering the helpful advice of Vicki in Ceduna, we started with the second of the five available. No sooner had we reached the cliff edge, when a young man in a red sports car screeched to a halt in the car park, jumped out and ran towards the cliff edge. Surely we weren't going to witness a suicide? He looked over and down at the surging sea, and galloped towards us.

'Do you know where I can get down there?' he asked with an intense urgency bordering on the fanatical.

'Are you kidding?' I gestured towards the vertical cliffs.

'There must be somewhere I can get down.' He said he had come from Western Australia, and had been checking all the lookouts as he headed east.

'Why do you want to get down there anyway?'

'Mate, just imagine the fishing! It has to be virgin territory. The fishing must be incredible! But I can't get down to try it.'

He said he was from Geraldton, where the fishing was very good. But he was sure it must be better under the cliffs of the Great Australian Bight.

'Maybe there's a chance at the next lookout. I think there's one more to go.'

Off he went in a cloud of dust.

'Ros, did I imagine that?'

We found the drive along the Nullarbor cliffs, with the Southern Ocean on our left, and flat treeless plains studded with saltbush and low scrub stretching to the horizon to the north, particularly exhilarating. Why do some people say the Nullarbor is boring? The border came into view conveniently at lunchtime and we pulled off the road to eat the last of our apples and bananas before we tackled the 'fruit and vegies police' at the border check. Even our Tasmanian leatherwood honey would have to go.

It is time to put our watches back 45 minutes for a time zone we didn't realise existed—Central Western Time. It is only enjoyed by a few hundred people in the eastern extremity of Western Australia, but when you slash off another hour for daylight saving (indignantly eschewed by Sandgropers as an eastern states impertinence) it all gets rather complex.

The agricultural inspector was firm but fair—although puzzled about how to inspect The Manor in its collapsed, travelling mode. Mercifully we did not have to crank it up to its camping height. The inspector managed to peer in through the side door and took our word that the fridge was fruit and veg free. We watched sadly as our Tasmanian honey was thrown unceremoniously in the rubbish bin, then headed towards Eucla which we reached by early afternoon because of the time change. Ignoring our body clocks which seemed to be telling us we needed a glass or two of red at 4.30 pm, we erected The Manor on the gravel surface of the camping ground, which overlooked the sand dunes that had eaten the original town of Eucla.

We are still up on the escarpment, but Eucla marks the place where the unbroken line of limestone cliffs around the Great Australian Bight retreats from the ocean, and the Eyre Highway drops down 87 metres to the plain behind the coastal sand dunes. To put off drinkies to a reasonable hour, we drove down to look at what was left of the Old Telegraph Station. Only two of its stone chimneys are now visible above the shifting sand dunes and they are photogenic but sad. The Telegraph Station and the small settlement around it were built as part of the Overland Telegraph Line linking Albany and Adelaide that was opened in 1877. Eucla could also be reached by sea, and remains of its jetty can still be seen on the beach nearby. At its peak, Eucla had a population of 70, with four streets of sandstone and wooden buildings—now all consumed by the shifting sand.

Why on earth would the telegraph authorities have built a town in a place where it would inevitably be eaten up by moving sand dunes? I could not find any information about this, even in the small, extremely interesting private museum attached to the Eucla Motel. I eventually found the answer on the back of a postcard of the Old Telegraph Station photographed when it could be seen in its full glory—rabbits! When the ubiquitous bunnies arrived they ate out the local vegetation and then burrowed down to eat the roots as well. The dunes moved in.

Situated on the border of Western Australia and South Australia, the Eucla Telegraph Station was a key link in the 2432-kilometre line. It was by far the busiest because of a farcical situation that existed before Federation. There were two Morse code systems and each state used a different one. The 90-minute time difference rigidly adhered to by the respective state telegraphists was only a minor inconvenience compared with the cumbersome way the station was run. W S Gilbert could scarcely have written a more ludicrous libretto. The state line was deemed to run down the centre of a long table in the telegraph office. On either side of a partition, operators in starched shirts, waistcoats, collars and ties sat receiving messages from their respective states and solemnly handing them across the table to their counterparts, for re-transmission by Morse key to the east or west.

The line was maintained by linesmen riding camels, and contact with the outside world was infrequent. Ships only called every three months or so. The Overland Telegraph Line was the only means of communication between South Australia and Western Australia for nearly 50 years until 1927, when it was replaced by a new line beside the transcontinental railway.

It is Ros's birthday and we have decided to celebrate with a night out at the Eucla Motel dining room. At 7 pm the sun is still up, and we sit beside a glass wall overlooking a remarkable courtyard garden. The desert has been made to bloom, with ornamental ponds and water flows supporting an eclectic mix of desert plants and unlikely offerings of roses, agapanthus, daisies, and nasturtiums. A ceramic fish just beside my right knee dribbles water from its open mouth. In the distance we can see the blue of the Southern Ocean, and the sprawling sand dunes. It is an extraordinary and unexpected oasis.

Edward John Eyre also found water in the sand dunes at Eucla, just in the nick of time. When he left the head of the Bight, Aborigines had told him that there was no more water on the cliff tops until some sand dunes could be reached—at least ten days' march in their terms. Eyre knew that Flinders' charts showed an unbroken line of cliffs for at least 200 miles from that point. Eyre and Cootachah, with two horses, set off ahead of Baxter and the others who were leading the packhorses and sheep. They hoped to travel faster and relay water back to the main party when they found it. In a journey fraught with risks, this was one of the biggest. After four days totally without water, their horses staggering and their own stamina failing, Eyre and Cootachah pushed on into darkness. When dawn broke on the fifth waterless day, Eyre saw the longed-for sand dunes beyond the line of cliffs ahead—but he also saw he had walked past some smaller dunes in the night.

Eyre was faced with an appalling choice. If he and Cootachah went back to the smaller dunes and found no water, they would not have the strength to reach the coast. Similarly, if there was no water at the furthest dunes, they would not be able to get back to where they were. Eyre pressed on towards a sandy shore in the distance. After some ten kilometres they came to a native path winding down a steep cliff to a beach with great white sandhills. There were Aboriginal wells and clumps of grass. 'Thus on the fifth day of our sufferings, we were again blessed with abundance of water . . .'

The next day Baxter, Wylie and Neramberein arrived safely with a line of very thirsty packhorses and sheep.

> The whole party were, by God's blessing, once more together and in safety; after having passed over one hundred and thirty-five miles of desert country, without a drop of water in its whole extent at a season of the year which is most unfavourable . . . the sheep had been six and the horses five days without water and both had been almost wholly without food.

They had arrived at the sandhills that Ros and I were overlooking beyond the splashing fountains and English roses of the Eucla Motel garden.

Over our steak and wilting vegies (which must have

come from the west) I toasted Ros and a great technological breakthrough. I had been wanting to access my e-mail, but could not do this from a public phone, because I needed to plug my Macintosh Powerbook into a phone socket. The motel office could not oblige, but suggested the service station nearby. The garage attendant listened to me as I described what I wanted and why, but boggled at words like 'computer', 'Internet', and 'e-mail'. He did, however, offer me the phone plug of his EFTPOS system, and while his customers waited, I managed to download my e-mail through a phone link to my service provider in far-away Perth. Appropriate, I thought, in view of the distinguished history of communications at Eucla.

Ros and I are continuing to debate whether we will head south to the coast from Balladonia, or continue on the Eyre Highway to Norseman. There is a road marked on the map, and all the serious four-wheel drive books rave about the delights of Israelite Bay, where there is an abandoned telegraph station—and unrestricted camping. The alternative is to drive south to Esperance from Norseman and then east again to reach the fabled Israelite Bay.

The problem with four-wheel drive enthusiasts is that so many of them are head-bangers. For them, there is nothing more exciting than putting their vehicles into extreme situations so they can use their rescue gear—snatch blocks, snatch straps, winches, kangaroo-jacks and all that. I have a winch, but I hope not to use it. Besides, we are towing The Manor which admittedly has off-road clearance, and we will be on our own. I wouldn't know a snatch block from a strap—even if I had one. Ros is nervous about attempting to get to Israelite Bay. Although

I am a four-wheel drive novice, I am gung-ho. This has nothing to do with red wine.

The discussion continues in the bar of the Eucla Motel. Richard, the barman, hears us mention Israelite Bay and tells us that the route south from Balladonia is rough but reasonably OK for most of the way—until the turn-off to Israelite Bay on a track which alternates between deeply trenched sand ruts and sharp tyre-tearing rocks. However, if we give Israelite Bay a miss and go straight on down to a town called Condingup, we will be close to our next destination, the Cape Arid National Park.

'The thing to do is to ask Max at the Balladonia Roadhouse. He'll tell you what state the road's in.'

I was curious why the obvious short cut down to the south coast was in such bad shape. According to Richard it was deliberate bastardry by the Norseman council, which allegedly kept the road a goat track so that all caravanners, campers and tourists heading for Western Australia would come to their town to fill-up with fuel, replace confiscated vegies, and then go south to the coast. We are still not sure what we will do. In any case that kind of ambivalence about where to go is half the fun of our kind of travel.

Next morning saw us rolling west by 7.30 am after an aspirin-assisted breakfast. I thought that was quite impressively early after the happy red-wine-fuelled celebrations of the night before and not much sleep due to fellow travellers inconsiderately deciding to up camp and move off at 3 am.

It is still unseasonably cool, and the countryside is mallee, mallee, and more mallee with an occasional saltpan lake glimpsed in the distance. The only human intrusions on to this landscape (apart from the road) are the roadhouses situated every 200 kilometres or so to refuel vehicles and travellers—Mundrabilla, Madura, Cocklebiddy, Caiguna, and Balladonia before the first settlement of any size at Norseman.

At certain intervals straight and level sections of the highway are marked out as emergency airstrips for the Royal Flying Doctor Service during floods. These only happen about once every ten years. (Later in our journey I met a flying doctor who had landed on one of these at night, illuminated only by car and truck lights at each end, and with a fierce crosswind blowing. He remembered it vividly.) And where else in the world would you be warned against hitting free-ranging kangaroos, emus and camels? All pictured on the same road sign, too.

We stopped at Caiguna for a bacon-and-egg roll and a soft drink. There we were not the only ones in need. A woman, who pulled up next to us with a car full of kids, practically fell out the driver's door holding a primed coffee plunger, and headed urgently towards a source of hot water and a caffeine hit. The Caiguna Roadhouse is fairly typical of the Nullarbor stops—simply a place to refuel vehicles and people. Some, like Caiguna, have a pub next door, others not. The roadhouses have a few magazines and souvenirs—otherwise the only service on offer is fast-food takeaway or eating at tables. There is no drama about crossing the Nullarbor these days on the bitumen, providing your vehicle is mechanically sound—there are no repair facilities between Ceduna and Norseman. The worst danger you have to guard against is falling asleep. Just after Caiguna is the Ninety Mile

Straight. Since metrication the '146.6 Kilometre Straight' doesn't have quite the same ring about it. So everyone still calls it the Ninety Mile Straight.

The walls of the Caiguna restaurant and takeaway are plastered with photographs, a cricket bat crudely fashioned out of a fence paling, sporting 'trophies' and other reminders of the 'Great Truckie Bog' in March 1995 when Cyclone Bobby unexpectedly flooded the highway or, more accurately, 21 kilometres of dirt-road diversion caused by road works on the Ninety Mile Straight. Some 1000 cars, trucks, semitrailers and road trains were stranded at various points between Norseman and Cocklebiddy—some in a sea of mud near Caiguna—for about two weeks.

The road works were to raise the level of the Eyre Highway so it couldn't be disrupted by rare flooding. Cyclone Bobby arrived at the wrong moment. Truckies, losing $1000 a day, were unamused but had to make the best of it. Drivers with their rigs up to the axles in soupy mud had to stay where they were. Others clustered around the remote roadhouses and organised cricket matches and card games to while away this outbreak of unexpected idleness. Adelaide truckie Bernie Dawe strung a tarpaulin between two bogged truck cabs and created a social shelter called 'Bernieville', where he companionably fried bacon, eggs, sausages and tomatoes.

At Norseman, where truckies clustered because they could not begin their eastern journey, there wasn't much else to do but drink. One truckie—who didn't drink beer because it made him aggressive—switched to rum and coke instead to be more sociable. Eventually he stumbled to his truck but couldn't find his keys to go to bed. So with boozy ingenuity he broke a side window to get in. The only trouble was, he'd picked the wrong truck. Its burly owner, also at that stage tired and emotional, was not pleased to find a stranger sleeping in his bed. He hauled the interloper out and belted him black and blue. Mostly though, stranded travellers were philosophical and good-humoured about it all. There wasn't much else they could do.

The ill-timed road work took place on the Ninety Mile Straight, which I was looking forward to driving along. There could have been longer straight stretches when the highway was rebuilt and sealed by 1976, but the designers deliberately built-in curves to try and combat driver fatigue. When the black-top was complete from east to west, the following exchange of correspondence was noted in the letters section of the Melbourne *Age* between C A Mullett and U R Fysh:

> Sir,
>
> Few people living in Melbourne this summer could have failed to observe that the tendency of Melbourne's weather to follow that of Perth by a few days as it usually does, has not occurred as it usually does.
>
> I have devoted a considerable time to investigation of this phenomenon, discussing it with an applied physicist and other informed people and performing complex meteorological calculations. I have concluded that the root cause for the breakdown in our weather patterns is the recent completion of the bitumen surfacing of the Eyre Highway across the Nullarbor. The basic mechanism behind this effect revolves around the black body radiation from the road surface causing thermal updraughts in an unbroken line across the continent . . .

The obvious solution is to paint the entire surface white to reduce the black body radiation and hence thermal updraughts . . .

C A Mullett

Sir,

I was most interested in the theory advanced by C A Mullett in his letter (27/1). My interest in the subject stems from my recent doctoral thesis in which I mapped the Nullarbor on a scale of 1:1. As the only place I could lay out my map was, naturally enough, on the Nullarbor, I had considerable occasion on which to study the Eyre Highway and the black-body phenomenon.

In my opinion Mr Mullett has overlooked two important factors—the curvature of the Earth and the speed of weather transfer. The sealing of the Eyre Highway has reduced the weather differential between the two cities to 53.5 hours (a reduction of 4.93 hours) . . .

The solution is to slow the weather to its former speed by installing 'speed bumps' on the highway . . . If painted white, [these] will also break the continuity of the black-body radiation and will be the world's longest pedestrian crossing in the Guinness Book of Records.

U R Fish

Ros saw nothing of the Ninety Mile Straight. She fell sound asleep.

five

Cocktails at Six

As I drove west along the Ninety Mile Straight at 110 kilometres per hour in airconditioned comfort, six-cylinder diesel engine humming smoothly and The Manor, well-stocked with food and water, following obediently behind, I thought again about young Eyre. It had taken us about four hours to drive the 400 or so kilometres from Eucla to Caiguna, but it took him almost two months to cover the same distance, during which time three of his horses and the Timor pony weakened and died of thirst—leaving only six horses and a foal. It was undoubtedly the most brutal and unforgiving sector of his westward journey. And there was worse to come.

Without their remaining packhorses they were as good as dead—it would be impossible to go forward to Albany, or back to Fowlers Bay—although the horses were by now carrying very little in any case. In their forced march along the top of the waterless cliffs, Eyre had found it necessary to abandon most of their equipment and supplies. Extra pack saddles, water kegs, buckets, most of their firearms, medicines and even their spare clothing had to go.

They had been saved on several occasions by finding native wells. The two young Aboriginal boys, Neramberein and Cootachah, had been riding on the strongest pack-horses during the day, until the horses became too weak even for that. Night marches were not possible because the boys did not have the physical stamina to walk through the day without a night's sleep.

By 9 April 1841 the party was camped on the coast, south from where Cocklebiddy is today. They were only halfway from Fowlers Bay to Albany. Baxter had been probing further west, but all five wells he had dug had yielded only salt water. Eyre was facing the ultimate reality: 'We had advanced into a country through which we could never retreat.' With 900 kilometres still to go, morale was at rock bottom.

Should they try to press on, or return to Fowlers Bay? They had buried some flour and supplies there, but it was highly likely those would have been found by local Aborigines—even if they could make it back so far. Agonising over what had become not exploration any more, but simple survival, Eyre was certain the best option was to push on. He believed that they would find good water and feed in better country Matthew Flinders had charted beyond the cliffs of the Bight. But even the utterly loyal Baxter was pessimistic, and argued that they should turn back. Eyre's earlier comments that they would reach Albany 'or perish in the attempt' could have been much on the overseer's mind.

Lack of food was not helping morale. On 16 April, Eyre shot a dying horse, its emaciated carcass was stripped, and the stringy meat salted and hung up to dry. They all gorged themselves, but Eyre and Baxter were violently ill. The meat was flyblown.

Baxter's mutterings and mumblings about his reluctance to go on had influenced the three Aborigines. By 20 April Eyre knew that someone had been stealing extra food from their combined rations, and accused the Aborigines. Wylie, and the older of the two boys, Neramberein, mutinied and said they would go on alone, believing it was their only hope of survival. The camp was an even gloomier one that night.

Eyre, Baxter and Cootachah decided to wait where they were for a few days in case it rained, because tantalising thunderstorms could be seen out to sea—but it never did. While they waited tensions between Eyre and Baxter increased. But on the night of 25 April, Wylie and a very sulky Neramberein came back to camp half-starved after four days on their own. Eyre welcomed them back, and provided some damper and tea. The five travellers were together again, but the atmosphere was poisonous, and the future still bleak.

On the evening of 29 April they stopped to camp, and Eyre decided to take the first watch, to make sure the horses did not wander too far during their grazing. He did not know it was a decision which would save his own life. It was a cold night, with a strong wind blowing in from the south-west. At 10.30 pm Eyre began to head the horses back to the camp to hand over to Baxter for the second watch. He was astonished to see a sudden flash in the distance, followed by the report of a gun. Eyre ran towards the camp to find Wylie running towards him crying out in great alarm 'Oh Massa, oh Massa, come here . . .' On reaching the camp, 'I was horror-struck to find my poor overseer lying on the ground, weltering in his blood, and in the last agonies of death'.

Baxter had been shot through the chest after he had discovered Neramberein and Cootachah plundering the food supplies. They were, after all, only kids who had panicked in the stress of the moment. Baxter died within seconds of Eyre's reaching him—and the explorer's utter despair is graphically chronicled in his diary:

> The horrors of my situation glared upon me in such startling reality, as for an instant almost to paralyse the mind. At the dead hour of night, in the wildest and most inhospitable wastes of Australia, with the fierce wind raging in unison with the scene of violence before me, I was left with a single native, whose fidelity I could not rely upon, and who for aught I knew might be in league with the other two, who perhaps were even now lurking about with the view of taking away my life as they had done that of the overseer. Three days had passed since we left the last water, and it was very doubtful when we might find any more. Six hundred miles of country had to be traversed before I could hope to obtain the slightest aid or assistance of any kind, whilst I knew not whether a single drop of water or an ounce of flour had been left by these murderers, from a stock that had previously been so small.

Eyre's first thought was for his own security. His double-barrelled shotgun had been taken by the fleeing Neramberein and Cootachah, and the only other rifle was unserviceable with a ball stuck in its barrel. He and Wylie gathered in the straying horses, and began to wait out a very long night. It was a low point from which it must have seemed impossible to recover:

> About midnight the wind ceased, and the weather became bitterly cold and frosty. I had nothing on but a shirt and a pair of trousers, and

> suffered most acutely from the cold; to mental anguish was now added intense bodily pain. Suffering and distress had well nigh overwhelmed me, and life seemed hardly worth the effort necessary to prolong it. Ages can never efface the horrors of this single night, nor would the wealth of the world ever tempt me to go through similar ones again.

The morning brought no comfort. Wylie lit a fire while Eyre assessed the remaining supplies, keeping a wary eye on the surrounding scrub. Baxter's surprising of the two boys had saved two-thirds of the supplies—18 kilos of flour, a little tea and 18 litres of water were left. The two serviceable double-barrelled guns were gone, together with tea, mutton, sugar and tobacco. Even so, Eyre now had to abandon all stores except 'the bare necessaries of life'—including his remaining books and instruments, collected specimens, and the last spare saddle.

Still unable to defend himself, Eyre determined to melt out the ball stuck in the barrel of his one remaining rifle. He placed it close to the fire, and nearly blew his own head off. Wet powder still in the gun suddenly discharged, the ball 'whizzing close past my head'. Eyre chastised himself for being so 'incautious', but felt a bit more secure with a working firearm. The ground was too stony even to accord Baxter the dignity of a burial. Eyre wrapped his body in a blanket, and left 'the melancholy scene accompanied by Wylie, under the influence of feelings which neither time nor circumstances will ever obliterate.'

Eyre could not be sure that Wylie had not been part of the original plot, although his sole remaining companion protested his innocence. If he were ambushed in the scrub by the two boys, Eyre decided he would have to shoot the elder boy, Neramberein. 'Painful as this would be, I saw no other alternative if they still persisted in following us.'

Late in the afternoon they saw Neramberein and Cootachah ahead, with the two stolen guns trained on them. But as Eyre advanced with his weapon at the ready, they fell back in distress and alarm. Eyre dropped his rifle and walked on unarmed. Shouting across the scrub he gave them stark alternatives. They could return eastwards along the coast towards Fowlers Bay—or be shot. The two boys called on Wylie to join them, but he stayed by the horses. Calling a final warning, Eyre and Wylie headed off. The two boys followed until they were outpaced by the horses, their pitiful cries finally dying away in the distance and gathering darkness. These were the boys in whom Eyre had earlier taken a fatherly interest.

It was typical of Eyre that as he agonised over what might have been—if he had not halted on the night of 29 April, or been so trusting after Wylie and Neramberein returned after the first desertion—he recorded very little animosity over the two boys who had murdered Baxter. They had obviously thought they were being led to their deaths, and knowing they could not survive from their hunting alone, panicked and decided to plunder the supplies. 'Nor would Europeans, perhaps, have acted better', Eyre wrote charitably.

No trace of the boys was ever seen again. Eyre knew that they were 100 kilometres from the nearest wells. They only had five litres of water and no horses to carry their supplies. It was unlikely they would survive even with their indigenous hunting skills. 'A dreadful and lingering death would in all probability terminate the scene, aggravated in all its horrors by the consciousness that they had brought it entirely on themselves.'

Meanwhile the Bowdens were approaching the first bend on the Eyre Highway for 146.6 kilometres since Caiguna. Negotiating it wakened my slumbering partner and alerted us to the imminent turn-off to Balladonia Station, where we had arranged to view the paintings of Amy Crocker (née Baesjou) who helped alert a grateful entomological world to the existence of the prehistoric ant *Nothomyrmecia*.

The homestead is close to the Eyre Highway and the ruin of an old Overland Telegraph Station, but cannot be seen because it is built behind a low outcrop of huge granite boulders. These boulders were good and bad news for the original pioneers. They formed natural tanks for the area's meagre rainfall, and were deepened later by camels dragging scoops, to make a succession of dams to sustain the settlement. The bad news was that the property was on a granite dome which ruled out the possibility of drilling bores for subartesian water. This was not known when the homestead was built in 1879.

We had made arrangements by phone from Eucla to see the art collection there—all paintings by Amy Crocker. Jackie Crocker welcomed us. She was on her own, apart from caring for an elderly boarder. Her husband John was away doing some contract carting. Jackie told us that things had never been drier. Until recently, there had never been a year when the property's dams and tanks had not carried them through. But several years ago it had not rained all year, so the Crockers gambled that this was a one-off and began carting water. It cost them $75 000—a debt they were still trying to pay off, and the reason John Crocker was away on the carting job.

Jackie, a cheerful, freckled redhead (who had been an English bride) said that they would not try carting water again. If the rain didn't come they would have to sell off their stock as the dams dried up. Who would be a farmer?

Jackie invited us in to see her mother-in-law's paintings, which covered the walls and central viewing panels of a large L-shaped room. Amy Baesjou (her family had Huguenot origins) had begun drawing and sketching as a small girl, and by the age of 17 was painting in oils. There are hundreds of paintings on display. Amy seemed to have painted every farm animal, cat and dog she ever owned. One unusual scene showed a camel grazing contentedly among a herd of Friesians. Each painting had a short description typed in block capitals by the artist. Sadly the camel—a family pet—had come to a sticky end, 'shot', wrote Amy with unconcealed fury, 'by a devil in human form in 1984'.

There is a kind of 'Grandma Moses' quality to Amy Baesjou's work. Some paintings are very successful, others less so, but they are always interesting. Much of her work recreates the pioneering history of the original properties in the region, depicting supplies being hauled ashore by camels from longboats on the beach at nearby Port Malcolm, with sailing ships standing off in the bay. The wool bales went out that way too. If Ros and I make it to Israelite Bay (the debate goes on) we can drive down to Port Malcolm which is nearby. It is a 'port' in name only, of course.

Ros was particularly interested in Amy's drawings of insects. Jackie noticed this and said that in Amy's later years, when she could not get out much, they would bring her insects they found on the property and say, 'I'll bet you haven't drawn this one'. And she would fossick around her collection and triumphantly produce the appropriate drawing. Surely, I said to Ros later, she must have drawn the prehistoric ant, *Nothomyrmecia*. Such a drawing has never been discovered.

Amy was still alive in 1975 during the filming of the ABC series, *Peach's Australia*. She was a woman of considerable presence and dignity, and her sangfroid was tested, according to Bill Peach, when his enthusiastic director—working as usual against the constraints of time and budget—was setting up the interviewing scene among the paintings. 'Now Bill, you stand here and, er, Thing . . . would you sit here . . .' Amy was deeply unimpressed. Bill thinks they were lucky not to be thrown out!

It was only a few kilometres' drive from Balladonia Station to Balladonia Roadhouse where the amiable Max held sway, dispensing fuel at 105 cents a litre for diesel (ouch!) and free local advice. Yes, the road south to Condingup was the way to go. 'The road gets better as you get further south.' He did not advise trying to get to Israelite Bay from this direction, but it might be less difficult once we got down to Condingup, and headed in along the south coast.

So the 'Great Israelite Bay Debate' goes on, but Ros is happy that we don't have to commit to it right away. We will not be going to Norseman. The town is named after a stockman's horse, we learned while looking at Amy's paintings. Seems a good enough reason for naming a town.

Max suggested we spend the night at old Deralinya

Station—an abandoned homestead which is gradually being restored for campers and travellers. He also gave us directions to follow bush tracks to another derelict historic homestead 20 kilometres or so to the east of Deralinya.

The dirt road south (the one allegedly neglected by the Norseman Council) was bad but not lethal. Penelope and The Manor sometimes achieved 80 kph, but longish sections were negotiated at 20 kph due to ruts, corrugations, awesome potholes and general uncertainty, although there was nothing that a conventional car could not have handled. Hairy chested, head-banging four-wheel-drivers would have been contemptuous of it. Still, it was good to see the stone walls of Deralinya Station and its outbuildings appear through the mallee around 6.30 pm. We erected The Manor just behind the quite well-preserved main building and there was even a tank with some fresh water as a bonus.

Inside the main room were a big fireplace, a rickety table, a wire mattress and some shelves with donations of ancient food, rusty kerosene lanterns, and battered pots and pans. There was also a grubby styrofoam cup containing small change and labelled 'Toilet Fund—initiated by various people who stop here. Please be honest.' We added a two-dollar coin and prepared to use our spade for essential purposes as the toilet renovations were still wishful thinking. Lighting fires outside in high summer was well and truly *verboten*, so we were delighted to be able to use the inside fireplace and Ros whipped up a damper in our trusty camp oven. I was the firemaster, but unfortunately the concentrated heat of the fireplace turned our first damper into a black projectile, reminding me of Ted Egan's song about the nefarious station cook

'Greasy Biggins' and his feared Biggins Buns—'the Anzacs could have fired them through their guns'. The second damper was simply superb. A light crusty brown, cooked right through, and delicious as toast smothered in Ros's home-made marmalade the next morning.

But that night we grilled some chops, opened a bottle of red, and sat by the light of our hissing Coleman lamp in front of the fire feeling that life could, indeed, be worse. The old homestead has a terrific atmosphere, and other travellers have reacted to it too. A card nailed above the chimney is inscribed: 'Travel is the art of always feeling at home.' Luke and Joan constructed a mock stone axe on 31 January 1996, on which they wrote: 'It is not what happens that determines our lives, it is what we do about it.' The old homestead seems to engender feelings of bush philosophy. The visitors' book makes good reading. Entry for 10 October 1997 (in a childish hand): 'We saw emu chicks very tame, Tonya had a blood nose, otherwise fine. Saw baby birds in nest in roof rafters, a snake near the loo, saw an eagle, two kangaroos, six emus, five horses and a foal.'

It is a small world. Ros has spotted an entry by John and Jackie Crocker, visiting from Balladonia Station. 'Nice to see Deralinya being done up. Amy Baesjou and her mother and father lived here in the 1920s. House was built by a Mr Scott for the Ponton Bros of Balladonia. Amy was the mother of John Crocker. Hope this history is of interest to fellow travellers. We would be happy to see anyone who is travelling east along the Eyre Highway . . . original painting of this house can be seen . . .'

It seemed churlish to rush away from such a splendid spot, so we decided to explore around a bit the next day and spend another night in Amy's childhood home.

Next morning I rigged up a bush shower over a gum-tree branch. It is axiomatic at these times that even if there have been no cars along for two days, one will appear. Ros managed her shower without interruption, but I had to make a naked and undignified dash from mine when a rather odd looking vehicle appeared from the south. It was an Australian-made Oka, a four-wheel drive which looked a bit like a cross between a World War II Bren-gun carrier and a small bus. It carried a group of about ten young people on an outback tour. They were a pleasant lot who reminded me of 1960s flower-power hippies. One young woman strolled over to the verandah of Deralinya, sat down and strummed on a musical instrument I had not seen before. I think she said it was called a *Mbara*—or something like that—from Africa. It was a series of steel keys, mounted on a board, which were flipped by the fingers of the player. The result was a percussive but charming melodious effect reminiscent of West Indian steel-drum music.

One of the young men wandered around the back where we had The Manor, climbed up a makeshift ladder and had a look in the battered corrugated-iron water tank. It was something I should have done earlier. The top was open to the birds, whose droppings had clearly enriched the water, the surface of which was covered in a rather unpleasant looking green scum. No wonder I have notched up three expeditions with the shovel today so far. I have been drinking the stuff unboiled.

Another young woman, Tessa Joy, swathed in tie-dyed saris and an air of serenity, has been travelling for the last seven years. She was very taken with Deralinya and delved in her cloth dillybag for some bibs and bobs with which she began to construct a kind of mobile from string, raffia, feathers, and some seashells. It took her about twenty minutes, and she hung her creation in front of the open window, where it twirled and spun in the breeze. I asked her about it.

'It's a dream-catcher.'

They finished their mugs of tea and roared off in the Oka. Ros agreed with me that it had seemed like a 1960s counter-culture time warp. I noticed Tessa Joy had written a whimsical entry in the visitors' book:

> 16/12/97. Just returned after three years' leave of absence—most disappointed to find Archibald has run off with the horses and Monique is nowhere to be seen. What's all this writing on the walls and can't he at least have cleaned the toilet? I'm a tad upset. I think I'll have a cup of tea.

What would Amy have made of it all?

The legendary Western Australian bushflies are a curse—small sticky and fearless, climbing into noses, eyes, and on all exposed skin, and riding if they can on forkfuls of food into open mouths. We have fly veils, and I put mine on over my brimmed bush hat and sit at a card table outside the homestead door writing up my diary on a portable eMate computer notebook. I hear a giggle, and there is a flash. Ros has taken my photograph. She said it is a bizarre sight. I can only agree—at first sight, an ageing, veiled, transvestite improbably writing in the bush.

The fly veils do keep the bushflies off but make eating, tea-drinking or involuntary nose-picking hazardous if you forget you have one on.

There are three dams at the back of the homestead,

and some scraggy fruit trees. Plenty of 'horsh' droppings around too, so there must be brumbies about and quandong seeds in the manure which suggest the horses must know where there are trees. We looked, but couldn't find any. There are rustic stockyards made from unsawn boughs still standing, and someone—perhaps one of the mysterious dunny renovators—has planted out a kitchen garden, protected by wire netting in which a few desiccated cauliflowers and gone-to-seed spinach plants are struggling for survival.

By midday it is hot and still, and a relief to drive off with Penelope's airconditioning on, to try to find Balbina Station about 20 kilometres to the east. Max at Balladonia Roadhouse had told us how to get there, across country. Just as we are wondering whether we are on the right track, we burst out of the mallee scrub into open plains, and see the small stone buildings that were once Balbina Station. As we begin to drive towards the remains of the settlement, about ten magnificent brumbies throw up their heads and gallop away across the dry brown grass, barely outrunning a startled emu which joins them in their flight.

It is good to see that something is being done to preserve these pioneering homesteads. There is a new roof on one of the barns, and the corrugated iron on the tiny homestead roof has been patched and worked on, although you can still see daylight in a number of places. Balbina Station was founded in 1893 by John Paul Brooks, described rather grandiloquently as 'gentleman, pastoralist, geographer' on a bronze plaque organised by the Brooks family. (Jackie Crocker told me that her mother-in-law Amy thought the Brooks's assumed airs and graces 'above their station'.) Brooks was born in 1840 and lived until 1930. He settled at

Port Malcolm on the coast in 1884 and was the first telegraph linesman at Israelite Bay before coming to Balbina. Brooks outlived his wife by twenty years, and his daughter (described on the plaque as 'pioneer, painter, botanist') by two years.

Returning to Deralinya felt like coming home. But there was no sign of Monique, and Archibald was still missing with the horses. As we enjoyed a cold beer, the gum trees framed a blood-red sunset. Tessa's feathered dream-catcher twirled lazily in the window. We must push on tomorrow, but it has been a wonderful interlude—particularly the luxury of having a fire at night.

The God of Camping turned on a short shower of rain as we were packing up to leave the next morning. Just enough to smear mud all over The Manor, and wet the canvas sidewalls as they were folded in over our beds.

South of Deralinya Station the road improved dramatically, particularly when we crossed into the shire of Esperance. We were back in wheat country for the first time since leaving the far west of South Australia. The vegetation was changing too. The road was lined by a variety of Western Australian *Banksia* we had not seen before. Both the scrub and cleared farmlands were ablaze with bright yellow flowering trees, known locally as Christmas bush, or more accurately *Nuytsia floribunda*, named after its discoverer, Dutch explorer Pieter Nuyts, who noted it in 1627 while sailing along the south-west coast of Australia.

So in our quest to follow the original explorers of this coast, we are now back in the seventeenth century. No wonder those who live in the west ponder in some paranoid perplexity about the east-coast delusion that Australian history began with Captain Cook. Pieter Nuyts' Christmas bush flowers only in December (of course) and is technically a parasite, which overcomes its grass host to proliferate in cleared paddocks as well as natural bush. We were right on the button to see its most spectacular display.

The wheat crop was being harvested, and a lumbering road train loomed up ahead, throwing up a great pall of white dust. After 15 minutes or so I became impatient and, as the road was straight, attempted to pass it. As I drew clear of the billowing dust and was able to see dimly I saw with horror another road train dead ahead, coming straight for us and barely 100 metres away. I plunged back into the dust, and Ros suggested gently (in a tone of voice she doubtless used in her nursing career to soothe lunatics) that it might be an idea if we stopped by the roadside, had a cup of coffee and let the road train get well ahead. This was excellent advice. Much better to stop, relax and have a cup of coffee and a biscuit than be dead.

We were heading down to a T-junction with Fisheries Road which runs east from Esperance about 30 kilometres inland from the coast, until it peters out into a four-wheel-drive-only track to Israelite Bay—now assuming iconic proportions in our thinking. First, though, we turned west for a few kilometres to Condingup which we hoped would provide some fresh supplies. It was the last fuel stop on Fisheries Road before Israelite Bay, and we needed that too. But we will spend the night at the Cape Arid National Park, about 100 kilometres east of Esperance.

The best the Condingup Store could do in the fresh fruit and vegies department was potatoes and onions, but we were pleased to see those—and a pack of frozen meat.

Cape Arid National Park is magnificent. The camping area is divided up into a series of bays among the brightly flowering *Banksia* overlooking the Thomas River inlet and lagoon, with a long curving white beach stretching around the bay towards distant granite promontories. Out to sea the horizon was broken by a number of granite islands, some with vegetation, some without. CALM (the Department of Conservation and Land Management) supplies a gas-fired barbecue, rough brackish water from a tank on a short tower, and a couple of well-built pit toilets, with concrete floors, and plenty of dunny paper. You pay an entrance fee to the park, but camping fees are voluntary.

We had the place to ourselves except for a caravan and an older Toyota four-wheel drive in the next bay—reminding us that the dreaded school holidays were imminent. As we walked down to the beach to check it out, we passed a couple and two small boys returning to their camp, and exchanged a few words. Not long after we expanded The Manor into camping mode, the younger of the two boys (he looked about six) arrived with a shy smile and a written invitation to 'Cocktails at six with the Williams—please bring your own glasses'. Well, why not!

Ros discovered that we had the fridge in The Manor running all day on gas, instead of 12-volt power from the Landcruiser. This was extremely dangerous and naughty, but thankfully all was well. The only minor disaster was leaking beetroot juice, which had escaped from a sealed plastic container and had not only permeated every single item in the fridge, but dribbled out the front and formed an obscene, blood-like puddle on the floor also staining a small cotton rug in front of the sink. It was remarkable that it had not reached our beds. One day scientists will discover the mysteries behind the all-pervasive qualities of beetroot juice—how and why it is not only able to insinuate itself through glass and plastic, but also then replicate itself and run wild, stain clothing and all inanimate objects within a square kilometre.

Greg Williams, Heather Messer and their two boys Todd (8) and Ryan (6) have been on the road for three years! They are from Woolgoolga in New South Wales, and just took off on a working holiday. Neither of the boys has ever been to conventional school. Heather teaches them with help from the New South Wales Distance Education Department program. The Williamses are also vegetarians. I never thought I'd become emotional about a salad, but when our 'cocktails' drifted seamlessly into a dinner invitation, we crunched happily into lettuce leaves, tomatoes and fresh capsicum. We'd only been on hard tack for less than a week! Heather also had Lebanese hommos dips, black olives and tofu.

Greg is a refrigeration engineer (and jack of many trades) by profession, but his real passion is landscape photography, which he hopes one day to practise full time. Meanwhile he works for several months at a time in towns to stock up the family fortunes, and then they take to the bush. They have come to Thomas River for Christmas mostly because of the remoteness and beauty of the place, but also because there are no camping fees. They are actually doing what many Australians dream of doing but never do.

We form one of those instant accords which can lead to firm friendship. (It did.) By the third glass of vino Greg and I are planning a combined expedition to Israelite Bay. We will take both Penelope and The Manor, while they will leave their caravan at Thomas River and camp in tents from their venerable Toyota Landcruiser. It is always safer to travel with someone, and Greg is one of those handy blokes who can fix anything from a car fridge to a broken axle. Or so it seems to me. He's probably got a welding outfit with him as well. I must remember to ask him. After a few more glasses absolutely anything seems possible.

After a head-clearing swim the next morning (even the ultra-dedicated Greg failed to make his customary 5 am photographic foray) we agreed that despite the vinous origins of our enthusiasm the night before, we really would go to Israelite Bay for one or maybe two nights, and began sorting out the gear we would take. The plan was to leave by lunchtime, as the school-holiday crowd was expected to descend on Cape Arid within two or three days. In fact the outside world started to arrive about 10 that morning when a Nissan one-ton utility with a strangely familiar white cabin drove past our camp. It had a distinctive stainless-steel beer barrel mounted under the rear of the tray. Ros twigged, just as the Nissan disappeared around the next corner of the sandy track.

'Tim—it's Ken and Liz from Fowlers Bay!'

I ran after them, but they had spotted us and came back. There was the customary 'What have you been doing since . . .', and we introduced them to Greg and Heather. Ken materialised with cold beers from the back of his truck and it seemed churlish to refuse. They were camped in their caravan further west, and were exploring the coast.

'We're just about to set off to Israelite Bay', said I with the false insouciance of an experienced four-wheel-driver. Ken and Liz both almost shrieked, 'Are you mad?'

Now Ken is as tough as they get, a South Australian farmer who recently handed over his property to his son to manage, and decided to take to the road for a bit of a break. His Nissan truck has all the four-wheel-drive essentials: winch, extra wire cable looped along the front of his bullbar, and God knows what else hidden away in the back of his cab. If a bush-smart bloke like Ken was spooked by going to Israelite Bay I was ready to listen.

He and Liz had set off the previous day. At the end of Fisheries Road, as advertised, the track became four-wheel-drive only. The narrow sand track was so deep they could barely see over the banks at either side. Not only that, the sand ruts were ridged with giant corrugations that almost shook their back teeth out.

'Mate, I'm telling you, it was diabolical. There were tree roots sticking out from the bank that would rip the sides out of your camper tyres. And then we hit the limestone. Fair dinkum, I thought I'd never make it. The point is, we couldn't have turned back even if we'd wanted to. So many four-wheel drives have been through there that the whole road is trenched down about a metre and a half.

'It took us two hours to go 17 kilometres. When we got to where we could turn around, we were so buggered we just had a cup of tea and turned around and came straight back.'

Greg Williams was looking thoughtful. I said: 'What was it like when you got to Israelite Bay?'

'That was the other thing—bloody awful.' Ken waved

his hand towards the glorious beach and blue ocean behind us. 'It's nothing like this. There are mangroves and bits of scrubby tea-tree, and the water is all muddy. Not only that, the four-wheel-drive campers who have been there have left great piles of bottles and garbage behind them. Why would you leave a beaut place like this to go to a dump like that?'

It seemed a pertinent question. While it was possible Port Malcolm to the south was more attractive, Liz and Ken were so traumatised by the drive in that all they wanted to do was get home.

It's funny how things sometimes work out. If we hadn't met Ken and Liz briefly at Fowlers Bay two weeks before, and if they had driven past our camp in the afternoon rather than the morning, we would have committed ourselves to Israelite Bay and the kind of deeply challenging four-wheel-drive experience we would rather leave to the hard-heads.

At least the 'Great Israelite Bay Debate' was finally over. What a relief. We don't have to go! Even a picnic at the dubiously named Poison Creek seemed a better option. But by the time our convoy of three four-wheel-drive vehicles reached Fisheries Road ready to turn west, Ken and Liz pulled over and stopped. An obscene mass of smoke was rising into the clear blue sky to the east—from where Ken and Liz calculated they were camped at Duke of Orleans Bay, so they said their farewells and headed back to check on their caravan. (As it happened the smoke was coming from an off-shore—fortunately uninhabited—island that had been somehow set on fire, and the whole thing was burned to a crisp. It looked as if a volcano had erupted.)

The Williamses and Bowdens continued for 70 kilometres along Fisheries Road, and then headed down to the coast. Before Poison Creek (I wondered if it had been named by Eyre, but was never able to find out) we passed Seal Point which offered shelter from the stiff southwesterly. Greg grabbed his spear (the family vegetarianism did not exclude fish) and became 'man the hunter'. Ros and I tried fishing off the rocks with our rods, but—surprise, surprise—did no good at all. Greg kept appearing with handfuls of green-lipped abalone and a surprising variety of succulent looking fish impaled on the prongs of his spear. He was delighted and so were Heather and the boys, eyeing off all that unexpected protein.

We did drive on to Poison Creek, but it turned out to be as attractive as its name—a shallow, black, unpleasant-looking lagoon snaking back behind sand dunes. As we headed back to Thomas River, Greg discovered the brakes on his 1980 vintage Landcruiser had failed. He decided to drive back without them, using his engine to slow down if he had to. All this went according to plan, but he got so confident that he forgot he had no brakes as he swung into his camp site, and nearly took out the caravan and happy home.

'Your brakes would have failed on our way to Israelite Bay if we'd gone', I reminded him. We celebrated not going by having a combined barbecue—the speared fish, abalone slices fried in garlic and ginger, and some singed cow courtesy of the Condingup store. Heather and Greg averted their eyes delicately from our meat-eating. I noticed Todd and Ryan sniffed appreciatively at the bits of burning beast—but they politely held the vegetarian line.

I told Greg and Heather about our interest in the early

explorers, and that our mixed grill was a distinct improvement on the one poor Eyre and Wylie endured while on their way to Israelite Bay and Port Malcolm, 157 years before us, after finally leaving the arid limestone cliffs of the Great Australian Bight behind them, and reaching reliable water. On 8 May, nine days after Baxter's death, Eyre and Wylie barbecued a dead horse which Eyre had shot just before the poor animal died of exhaustion anyway.

Wylie was a formidable trencherman. As Eyre began to skin the carcass, Wylie grabbed a piece of the flesh as soon as he could, and began alternately singeing and eating it.

> After cutting off about 100 pounds of the best of the meat, and hanging it in strips upon the trees until our departure, I handed over to Wylie the residue of the carcass, feet, entrails, flesh, skeleton, and all to cook and consume as he pleased, whilst we were in the neighbourhood. Before dark he had made an oven, and roasted about twenty pounds to feast upon during the night.

I thought it was important Heather and Greg should be aware of this.

They were both aware of Eyre's epic journey, and when the little boys were in bed, we sat under the stars and talked about Eyre and Wylie's situation after leaving the Bight and before they reached Thomas River.

By then Eyre knew they would probably survive, although they still had more than 600 kilometres to negotiate before Albany. But water was no longer such a problem, and there was better feed for their few remaining horses. However, it was also winter, and bitterly cold.

Heather was interested in the relationship between Eyre and Wylie at that time, after the murder of Baxter.

'Immediately after Baxter's murder, Eyre was very worried about Wylie's loyalty. After all, he'd deserted him once already. But he also knew that Wylie could have left him when they confronted Neramberein and Cootachah the day after the murder, and he didn't.'

Another clue to the changing nature of what had become a partnership of survival was the way Eyre referred to his Aboriginal companion. Before the murder, he rarely called him Wylie—usually writing 'the King George Sound native' in his journal. But after the terrible events of 29 April, he simply refers to him as Wylie, and as the weeks go on, his journal reflects not only increasing regard and respect for Wylie, but warmth and friendship.

Port Malcolm, near Israelite Bay, was an important staging post for them. They rested there while Eyre caught crabs and fish from the rocks (he nearly got swept away by a rogue wave) and the horses grazed on the same good, green pasture that would later be enjoyed by the stock of the Baesjou and Brooks properties.

Eyre did not cross the Thomas River at the sandbar below us, but further inland. He camped by it on 29 May (exactly a month since Baxter's death)—the first flowing fresh water he had seen since leaving Adelaide! That night he and Wylie enjoyed a good dinner of roasted possum.

We toasted them both, and slept.

six

Lucky Bay, Wind Farms and Space Junk

The camp, company and location at Thomas River, Cape Arid, is simply too good to rush away from. We will spend another day and night before heading west to Lucky Bay and Esperance. Besides, we are enjoying our time with the Williamses.

Freed from the challenge of Israelite Bay (how will I ever be able to hold up my head in four-wheel-drive circles when this gets out!), Greg suggests we drive around the beach of Yokinup Bay towards the Cape Arid Peninsula. Now I have to confess that I have never done such a thing. As a native-born Tasmanian, I carry deeply entrenched prejudices about driving on beaches. The sight of a four-wheel-drive vehicle on a Tasmanian beach is about as welcome as an ex-husband at a wedding. Yet I am also aware that driving on beaches is a deeply entrenched part of what Tasmanians call 'mainland' culture. Provided beach drivers do not hoon about on the dunes, the area between high and low tide is—as I have been told by beach-driving enthusiasts—a wonderful stretch of potential highway, with all evidence of tyre tracks removed by the good Lord with every tide.

Ros is not completely happy about doing this, and asks pertinent questions about the state of the tide. The little boys, Todd and Ryan, think it is a marvellous idea, and the two Landcruisers begin a stately convoy along the beach. Both Greg and I know our tyres are too highly inflated for beach driving, and when the beach narrowed after about four kilometres we headed up into the softer, higher sand until we ground to a halt. The trick, apparently, is to swing the nose of the vehicle up the beach at these times, so you can reverse down the slope to turn. I did the opposite. But what the books say is right. Once the tyre pressures were drastically reduced we got going again, but this time heading home. Greg still didn't have any brakes, and he felt he ought to fix them. Heather agreed! Ros also pointed out the tide was definitely coming in, and the beach was becoming even more narrow.

I was anxious to enlist Greg's help to get our car fridge working again. The young man in Sydney who installed the 12-volt power outlet in the rear section of Penelope had done so in a way that meant if the fuse ever blew—which it just had—you had to practically demolish the whole car to get at it. Well, that is an exaggeration, but to take the side panel out and uncover the fuse meant dismantling the luggage platform and heavy-duty drawers packed with tools, jacks and extra gear. I did the donkey work and Greg was able to fix the fuse and relocate it so it could be got at without doing all that ever again. It only seemed to take him minutes to fix his brakes. Not being a practical bloke, it seems to me that Greg can fix absolutely anything. We are most grateful. Fancy camping next to a refrigeration engineer! (I found out later that he pumped up the hydraulic pressure in his brake lines with a 50/50 mix of brake fluid and a $2 bottle of muscat we had generously given the Williamses, purchased at a winery near Barmera in South Australia. Six months later the brakes were still working perfectly. Perhaps the winery concerned might like to use it in their advertising?)

Greg even had time to go spearfishing around the rocks before lunch, and claimed to have nearly speared a mighty fish that might have fed them for a week. There was the obligatory chorus of disbelief.

Over lunch we quizzed Heather and Greg over how they had managed to realise a lifestyle that most couples with young kids only dream about. It all started when Greg and Heather went for a holiday in Sulawesi, Indonesia, in 1994. At that stage Heather was a TAFE teacher working between Grafton and Coffs Harbour, New South Wales, while Greg was managing a wholesale refrigeration and airconditioning business in Coffs Harbour.

'We were raising two children and trying to owner-build our house', said Greg. 'In a word—stress!'

Heather said that the people in the part of Sulawesi where they were holidaying were known as the 'Smiling Minahasen', a name given to them by the colonial Dutch, because of the resilience and good nature of this physically attractive race. During their two-week holiday, Greg and Heather wondered how the smiling Minahasen could be so happy with so little material wealth. 'Our conclusion was that western society has got it wrong', they said.

Greg's mind was further concentrated by turning 40, 'which made me consider my own mortality and how I could head towards the things I wanted to achieve in life. Sitting at home and wishing I was a great landscape photographer was not the way to achieve my goals.'

Heather and Greg had done a round-Australia trip in 1988 and were no strangers to camping and travelling. But now they had children who had to be educated. Their family and friends were generally dismissive of their plans.

Heather found a vastly different attitude when she and Greg visited the Distance Education Department at Casino Public School. 'What struck us was the enthusiasm and acceptance of what we were planning, whereas even our schoolteacher friends were pessimistic about Todd's and Ryan's educational future.

'It was a strange experience to walk into a room where several teachers were having quite animated discussions with invisible students. They were actually making audio tapes to be mailed away to them.'

Being on the receiving end of this process is virtually a full-time job for Heather. Every week Todd and Ryan each receive a package which has a set period of work, reading material, books and audio tapes, and Heather supervises their daily schooling. About once a week, if possible, the boys talk to other remote-area students on a conference phone. Sometimes Greg has to drive them to a mountain top to get reception on his mobile phone.

Both parents are delighted with the way the two boys are progressing. On their 1988 trip, Greg was appalled at the trouble other travellers went to in order to receive television—even to the extent of having satellite dishes strapped to the back of their caravans.

'One evening I remember Heather, myself and a

handful of travellers enjoying a camp fire, a lively chat, and a beautiful star-filled sky, while every other caravanner was locked inside getting their hit of television.'

They made a deliberate decision not to take a television when they left Woolgoolga, and the boys are essentially growing up without it. This, their parents are convinced, has done wonders for their imagination. Ros and I had noticed their ability to play together happily for hours at a time, using a few stones or shells to augment their toys and chattering away to each other. They seemed to have an instinctive appreciation of their natural surroundings.

Greg said they did go to a formal school for a term while he was working in Perth. On Ryan's first day, the six-year-old chose to eat his lunch up a tree. 'This was not normal and acceptable behaviour, according to his teacher. What crap!'

However, at the end of the term Todd's teacher commented that it was refreshing to meet a boy who was untouched by commercialism and who obviously spent a lot of time with his father. Greg was delighted.

Heather said that if they ever wrote a book about their travels it would be called 'You're So Lucky'—which is what strangers generally said about their lifestyle.

'But we're not lucky—we just did it!'

A father with two children slightly younger than Todd and Ryan joined us at the communal Thomas River barbecue. Mike was a medico with the Flying Doctor Service. He had come down to Thomas River from Kalgoorlie, a few days ahead of his wife who was a remote-area nurse. They were an English couple who had applied for their jobs from the Old Dart. Mike was clearly grateful that there were other kids to play with for his two, who were a bit of a handful. I asked him about the emergency airstrips we had seen marked out on the bitumen of the Eyre Highway and whether he had ever had to land on one.

'They only get used when wet weather closes all the other strips, and in this part of the world that's about once every ten years. I did have to use one for an emergency during the aftermath of Cyclone Bobby in 1995 when all those trucks and cars were stranded near Caiguna', he said.

'I'll never forget it. There was a crosswind, it was at night, and the only lights we had were cars with their headlights at each end. The pilot did a great job to get us down safely—but it was hairy.'

At that moment a familiar white Nissan truck pulled up, and Ken and Liz arrived—Ken clutching six-packs of cold beers in his weather-beaten hands. It was going to be one of those days. Besides, we had not celebrated with them for sparing us the ordeal of Israelite Bay. I said to Ros that if we didn't get away the next morning we'd settle in for the summer.

The decision to leave was not helped by another glorious morning on the south-west coast with a cobalt blue Southern Ocean creaming itself on to the pure white sand of the beach below. But we don't have unlimited time on our westward journey.

Greg had been up at sparrowfart as usual with his camera to capture the dramatic Cape Arid landscape in the soft early morning light. The coastal *Banksia* around our camp was festooned with fresh golden globes, while new growth speckled the duller green of the old foliage with a dusting of silver. A screeching cluster of cheerful black cockatoos were doing rusty-hinge imitations and tearing at the older *Banksia* cones when Heather came by to see how we were going with our packing up.

'Where's Greg?'

'I'm not allowed to tell you this', said Heather conspiratorially, 'but you know that big fish he was talking about yesterday that he jagged with his spear but got away? Well when I was jogging along the beach this morning, I saw the seagulls clustered around something—and it was the same fish washed up. I could see the spear marks on its side. Greg feels awful about it, and has gone down to bury it. He doesn't want you to know, so I haven't said anything . . . right?'

We collapsed The Manor and stowed our gear, in no hurry to leave this most favoured of camp sites. Greg and the two small boys, appeared looking sheepish, or perhaps fish-ish. Our farewells were genuinely sincere. You meet many pleasant people on camping journeys, but occasionally you come across individuals you know instinctively will become lifelong friends, if the tyranny of distance allows. As the Williamses were heading west also there was a good chance we could see them again at Albany and we made plans for that. We nibbled Heather's almond cookies as we juddered over the corrugations heading out of the Cape Arid National Park.

With only a half-day's run to reach Cape Le Grand National Park and the Lucky Bay camping ground we motored at a leisurely pace through the low *Banksia*-rich scrub, noting sadly that many *Banksias* were dying. This is due to the scourge of die-back, unwittingly introduced to Western Australia from Asia probably more than a century ago. It is the slow-acting fungus *Phytophthora*. Plants die when the fungus attacks their roots, preventing them from absorbing water and nutrients. *Banksia* is particularly vulnerable, and often the first sign that die-back is at work. It has been spread over the years by human activity, by agricultural machinery, boots and car tyres.

The Department of Conservation and Land Management has closed some four-wheel drive and walking tracks in the national parks to try to contain the inexorable spread of *Phytophthora* but unfortunately it is only containment and not a cure. Where tracks are open, CALM has put stiff brushes and metal trays where walkers can brush their boots before and after walking on park trails.

To our eastern-states eyes, the vegetation of the south-west of Western Australia is markedly different. Ros, who has nearly finished a three-year horticulture course, is in a constant state of almost orgasmic botanic delight.

As we turned south again to run down to the coast, and the camping ground at Lucky Bay, we passed a spectacular granite feature, Frenchmans Peak—well-named because its top is crowned by a huge slab of rock, looking very like a Gallic beret worn at a rakish angle. Frenchmans Cap would have been a more apt moniker. 'We'll climb that later', I said cheerfully. Ros looked faintly apprehensive. She likes walking, but feels no compulsion to climb mountains.

At Lucky Bay the prevailing south-westerly was screaming through the stunted trees and flapping the annex canvas and tents of already established campers. It seemed almost a full gale, but at least Lucky Bay was sheltered. On the obligatory white sandy beach, only a few metres from the camping ground, anglers sat on deckchairs while the offshore wind obligingly carried their lines out into the translucent water, almost iridescent green close in, merging to the deepest of blues out in the bay, protected by great smooth granite outcrops to the south-west. Out to sea the white caps were racing each other furiously further east.

Conditions were probably much the same when Matthew Flinders called by in 1802. On 5 January Flinders had sailed from King George Sound, and soon sighted the Archipelago of the Recherche, a vast conglomeration of islands, rocks and shoals, stretching east from Esperance Bay for nearly 150 miles. These islands had been already sighted by the Dutch explorer Nuyts in 1627, and in 1792 by the French explorer Admiral D'Entrecasteaux who had landed on one of the islands. But both explorers had given the obvious dangers of the archipelago a wide berth. Flinders was well-aware of the hazards but took on the challenge in order to get to the coast, which he could not otherwise properly chart. The weather was fair, with a moderate breeze from south-south-east, as he sailed *Investigator* between the many rocky islands ahead.

Sailing towards an uncharted shore through rocky hazards was not recommended procedure even for pioneering navigators far from home. On 9 January Flinders landed on Remark Island and from the top of its rocky peak took bearings to fix the positions of the many other islands he could see. By late afternoon the ship was off Mondrain Island some miles to the east. But there was no clear water in which *Investigator* could stand off during the night, and the islands offered no shelter. Flinders discussed the situation with his sailing master, John Thistle, and made a decision even he admitted was dangerous. They steered straight for the mainland, where he had noticed some sandy beaches, and by 7 pm entered a small bay, sheltered from almost every direction. They had been lucky, and so named Lucky Bay. They were lucky in other ways, too, as their naturalist Brown collected more than 100 botanical species. Flinders visited Mondrain Island and discovered the Recherche rock wallaby. His party also lit a fire which burnt out the entire island.

There wasn't much shelter for The Manor at the Lucky Bay camping ground when I wound her up and extended our beds. There was certainly no point in putting up the awning. We'd have become airborne. We had a cuppa while our happy home bucked and flapped in the howling wind, and I saw the park ranger coming by. 'How long has this wind been like this?' 'Oh, about a month', he said. 'It's always like this at Lucky Bay at this time of the year.'

We put on our parkas and headed back over a low, scrub-covered hill towards Thistle Beach. Just behind it is a freshwater lagoon which helped sustain Eyre, Wylie and their remaining horses in 1841. Eyre knew the water was there, because Matthew Flinders had charted the coastline and had named Thistle Beach (with its abundance of fresh water) after his ship's master who had put ashore there. In fact at this stage Flinders was following up on territory first charted by D'Entrecasteaux—to give him his full name, Rear Admiral Joseph-Antoine Raymond de Bruni D'Entrecasteaux (I think such a name thrust greatness upon the owner), who had stooged along this part of the coast with his two ships *Le Recherche* and *L'Espérance* in 1792.

At the top of the hill we looked down on Thistle Beach, with the darker blue of the freshwater tarn behind, its surface corrugated by the relentless gale. I had been rabbiting on about the history of the place and not concentrating on navigation. The track we thought we were following wasn't all that well-defined. It was late afternoon and Ros, whose appetite for scrub-bashing off established tracks is nonexistent, asked me rather acidly if I expected to be back at camp by dark.

Beyond Thistle Beach we could see the looming bulk of Cape Le Grand further west, named after one Citizen Le Grand, a crewman of the French expedition. Flinders had deliberately headed towards this coast, despite the navigational nightmare presented by strong winds, and a conglomeration of uncharted islands and shoals. But in 1792 D'Entrecasteux's two ships were being driven east without choice, having sheltered at Esperance Bay further west. They were in great danger, being driven inexorably towards the coast by a rising gale. On board *L'Espérance* the intrepid Citizen Le Grand (this was not long after the French Revolution and 'citizen' distinguished between royalist officers and republican crew) climbed to the masthead 'in the midst of the tempest' and pointed out the anchoring place in which he was certain both ships could ride in safety.

His action saved the two vessels. When both were riding safely at anchor in the shelter of the cape, Le Grand was rowed across to the flagship to be presented to his generously named commander. Admiral D'Entrecasteaux kissed him on both cheeks and said, 'We owe you our lives.

'Sooner or later we shall pass away, but to you I give

immortality. Yonder Cape shall bear your name on the charts of this land for all time.'

Ros said, 'I'm pleased for Citizen Le Grand, but are we going to try to find the track or go back the way we came?'

'I'm sure the track must be near here somewhere. But there's more. Wait till I tell you what happened to Edward John Eyre when he arrived in these parts.' My partner usually has a fine sense of history, but now she seemed oddly distracted.

By the time they reached Lucky Bay, Eyre and Wylie were surviving on the dried flesh of their dead horses, and an occasional kangaroo. On good days they managed to catch some fish or crabs. Wylie was a prodigious eater when there was tucker available. One evening Eyre watched fascinated as Wylie scoffed 'a pound and a half of horseflesh, some bread, then the entrails, paunch, liver, tail and hind legs of a kangaroo, followed by a penguin he found dead on the beach'.

'He then made a little fire, and laid down to sleep, and dreamed of the pleasures of eating; nor do I think he was ever happier in his life.'

By the time they were approaching Lucky Bay their diet had been expanded to include the boiled root of the flag-reed, which 'when roasted in hot ashes, yields a great quantity of a mealy farinaceous powder'. Wylie had also found lots of witchetty grubs in the stumps of rotting grass trees, but Eyre could not bring himself to try those.

By that stage, Eyre knew that he and Wylie would probably survive to reach Albany, but it would be bush tucker all the way. What was about to happen near 'Lucky' Bay was beyond his wildest imaginings. As he and Wylie neared what would later be called Rossiter Beach to the east of the bay, Eyre was elated to see a most unexpected sight—a small boat. They pushed on, but lost sight of it behind a rocky outcrop. It appeared again, and then they saw a second boat.

With frantic haste, Eyre and Wylie made a fire, waved, fired shots and tried everything they could think of bar telepathy to attract attention, but the boats sailed on. As they watched, the sails came down, and they appeared to be fishing. They were whaleboats, so Eyre was sure there must be a whaling ship nearby. They scanned the horizon and saw a mast behind some rocks some distance away.

The thought of more food had Wylie making little cries of joy and skips of delight. Eyre was no less excited until the awful thought struck that this opportunity might sail away. Leaving Wylie, Eyre mounted the strongest horse and rode further along the coast. From a cliff top he saw a fine barque sheltered in a bay. The crew were peacefully cleaning ropes, but Eyre's waves and shouts were still not heard. Wylie caught up, and the two men made a fire and kept hailing. To their delight a boat put off towards the shore. A few minutes later, Eyre was shaking hands with the English master of a French whaler, *Mississippi*, Captain Rossiter.

While the horses were left to graze, Eyre was transplanted from the most basic hardships to the epicurean splendours of European luxury. Captain Rossiter put everything the travellers could want in front of them, and Eyre was dazed at the unreality of the transition. The French sailors were amazed at Wylie's ability to wolf down prodigious quantities of ship's biscuits. Later, lying in a dry bed, listening to the wind roaring and the rain beating against the timbers (it was midwinter by then and almost a year since he had set out from Adelaide) Eyre could not sleep. He thanked God 'for the inexpressible relief afforded us when so much was needed, but so little expected'.

Eyre spoke French quite well, and got on amicably with the young French sailors. Wylie's enormous appetite became the ship's source of amusement. Captain Rossiter took Eyre ashore and showed him peas and potatoes he had planted, and to an island where a collection of pigs, tortoises and Madagascan sheep were kept. *Mississippi* had been in the Cape Le Grand area for three weeks, but had seen no whales in that time. Eyre and Wylie enjoyed Rossiter's hospitality for twelve days. It was an incredible interlude.

On 14 June a large supply of stores was landed for the two explorers. Forty pounds of flour, 6 pounds of biscuit, 12 pounds of rice, 20 pounds of beef, 20 pounds of pork, 12 pounds of sugar, tea, a Dutch cheese, 5 pounds of butter, 2 bottles of brandy and even 2 saucepans—plus a pipe and tobacco for Wylie. The generous captain also presented Eyre with 6 bottles of wine. It was a considerable improvement on the rank, dried horse meat and flag-root they had been surviving on before meeting the good ship *Mississippi*. Their journey to King George Sound was now assured.

Our hike to Thistle Beach, however, was not. The track had wilfully disappeared, so we scrub-bashed down to the parking area on top of the beach (Ros was muttering softly) and decided to walk back around the road to Lucky Bay while there was still daylight—a longer journey but easier walking.

Snug inside the wind-buffeted camper, we fired up some spaghetti bolognaise and a glass or two of red, and an added luxury that Eyre and Wylie could not have enjoyed with Captain Rossiter—a battery-powered CD player enabling pianist Daniel Barenboim to thrash away splendidly at Beethoven's 'Appassionata' sonata. As Ros sagely remarked, 'Camping is not about deprivation, but indulgence'. Explorers worked the other way.

All night the wind shrieked and howled and flapped the canvas side walls of The Manor, the stronger gusts bending the telescopic arms of the roof supports in dramatic fashion. But like the three bamboos of Japanese mythology bending against the typhoon, the flexing was within design limits. We both find strong winds hassling, and there seemed no reason to hang about. When you have a camper like ours, packing up in a strong wind is interesting, but by 9 am we had tamed our canvas and closed down the roof into travelling mode.

We are bound for Esperance, not far from here and the biggest town we will have experienced since leaving Port Augusta. We are heading for fresh fruit and vegetables, lacking (apart from plundering the Williams) since the West Australia border vegie police confiscated all ours ten days ago.

On our way out of the national park we climbed Frenchmans Peak. It was a steep scramble up weathered granite, but not dangerous. Just below the summit there is a spectacular view of the surrounding countryside and coast through a great cleft that wind and erosion have made right through the mountain, under the Frenchman's beret which is a huge slab of tilted rock topping the mountain and on top of which is the actual summit.

There is a 360° view to be enjoyed there, if you can stand up. The famous Lucky Bay prevailing wind was whipping wisps of cloud about our ears. It was cold, and there was no incentive to linger. Ros found it necessary to piddle on the Frenchman's head, but I waited until the region of his eyebrows and shelter from the wind before I marked out my territory.

Esperance is but a hop, skip and a jump from Cape Le Grand and the Williamses had whetted our appetites by describing delicious tortes and homemade pies to be had at Merrivale Station on the way in to Esperance. We carefully timed our arrival at lunchtime, and our salivary glands began juicing at the gate where there was an enormous brightly coloured replica of a black forest cake. Sadly, on the shut gate to the property a few metres further on there was a sign saying CLOSED TILL BOXING DAY.

It is strange to see traffic lights and roundabouts. Esperance is named after one of Admiral D'Entrecasteaux's two ships. The Admiral was blown past the splendid anchorage of King George Sound in a storm, but managed to put in to Esperance Bay in 1792 to repair *L'Espérance* shortly before committing his ships to another tempest—from which they were saved by the keen eye of Citizen Le Grand. While fixing the ship in Esperance Bay, Monsieur Riche, the expedition's naturalist, wandered off looking for specimens and was presumably so carried away by the excitement of new discovery that he got himself lost for two days and had to be rescued by his shipmates.

During his wanderings he discovered the famous Pink Lake, and a spectacular iris-like wildflower which was named *Anigozanthus manglesii*—known now as kangaroo-paw and which has become the national flower of Western Australia. The Pink Lake is coloured by salt-resistant algae and we didn't think it was very pink when we saw it in the early afternoon. Perhaps early morning or evening is a better time. The colour does vary, according to the local literature, from pink to purple. And perhaps photographers working for tourist brochures used filters to pink it up a bit? Perish the thought.

We established ourself on a nice patch of green grass in a waterfront caravan park and luxuriated in hot showers, the convenience of washing machines, and the chance to catch up with our mail for the first time since leaving Sydney. There are supermarkets here, and it is time for resupply. It is also time for some forward planning. We still have not decided where to spend Christmas—now only a few days away.

A young couple, Alison and Paul, are camped in a tiny tent next to us. They are operating out of the boot of their small sedan car of doubtful pedigree, and are driving around Australia. Compared with us, they are minimalist campers. Apart from their flimsy tent, they have a double air mattress, folding table, a stool and a chair and a little one-burner gas cooker. They are still bubbling with enthusiasm after six months on the road. They work when they have to, to stock up the piggy bank for fuel and food, and hope to keep on keeping on as long as possible before reality catches up with them. It is not only grey power that is on the road. How dare the young have fun too!

After lunch and reading our letters we went shopping for maps, and I had a manly talk with the bloke at the auto spares shop about greased trailer balls. Ros thinks I should be greasing the tow ball, but I have plumped for a dry ball until now. The auto spares man wasn't keen to weigh into this domestic dispute, but said he greased his own ball. So I said I'd grease mine too. That settled, we returned to camp with our maps. You can't have too many maps on a trip like this; it's good to have continuing debate and dialogue about where to go.

At least we have worked out where we will spend Christmas. Our next area of exploration is the Fitzgerald River National Park, on the coast, about 200 kilometres west of Esperance. On its eastern boundary is Hopetoun, a small hamlet with a historic pub (always good to hear about), legendary beach fishing (we will see) and, essential for our immediate purposes, a caravan park and camping ground. I phoned the manager and said we hoped they had 'room at the inn' on Christmas Eve and, if not, could we lodge in the stables because my wife was heavily pregnant . . . She responded with appropriate drollery and said we could have a powered or an unpowered stable. That settled, Ros and I tootled off in Penelope to explore Esperance.

In modern times Esperance has become the port for the Kalgoorlie goldfields and a place where the mining families head to for the beach and a summer break. After our old friend Admiral Bruni D'Entrecasteaux called in (I feel he is an old friend, because he also explored around the coast of Van Diemen's Land and has a channel and an island named after him) the only European activity was rather wild and woolly. The offshore islands and parts of the coast near Esperance were the stamping ground in the 1830s of sealers who were mostly ex-convicts from Van Diemen's Land and French and American whalers. They sustained themselves on the Cape Barren geese, local kangaroos and abundant fish, and reputedly robbed and murdered each other when not otherwise occupied butchering whales.

The first permanent settlement at Esperance was in 1863 when the Dempster brothers, Andrew, Charles and William, trekked over from Northam (just east of Perth) with sheep and cattle to try their luck on a land grant awarded them in 1863. The Overland Telegraph Line came through in 1876. But it was the discovery of the goldfields around Kalgoorlie in the 1890s that really kick-started Esperance, which became an important port for the goldfields, and was declared a town in 1893. However the building of a rail link in 1909 from Perth to Coolgardie and then on to Norseman dealt a savage blow to the Esperance economy and things stayed fairly sleepy for almost half a century.

There was a puzzle, you see. The country around Esperance looked fertile. The soil was sand and loam, lightly wooded, with a reasonable rainfall. It seemed the kind of country where sown wheat should have sprung up and hit the farmer under the chin, and sheep and cattle could safely and profitably graze. But all efforts to extend agriculture were a disaster. Crops did not grow as they should, and cattle and sheep withered away and died even when there was plenty for them to eat. It took until 1949 for the CSIRO to find out what was amiss—the soil was deficient in important trace elements like copper, cobalt, zinc or molybdenum. A few handfuls of these per hectare and a superphosphate, and the problem was solved.

American interests became terribly excited by all this

after Harold Holt (then Liberal Minister for Labour) addressed a dinner in California touting the advantages of investing US capital in Australia. An investment group called the Allan Chase Syndicate was formed—nicknamed the 'Hollywood Pioneers' because of some of the high-profile entertainers involved, like Art Linkletter and Rhonda Fleming. Their first Australian venture, a rice-growing project in 1955 at Humpty Doo in the Northern Territory, was scuppered by a lack of flood control in the Wet, and the voracious appetite of the local magpie geese. Then the Administrator of the Northern Territory, Frank Wise (a former premier of Western Australia), turned the attention of the Hollywood Pioneers south-west to his home state and the sand and mallee hinterland of Esperance.

In 1956 some 607 000 hectares of land were sold to the Americans, half of which was to be cleared and cultivated and sold off as blocks to settlers. The recommended time to develop this grade of land and soil from virgin bush to pasture in Australia is around three years, but the Americans thought they could do it faster—in one. Alas, the combination of haste, greed and unseasonable low rainfall created a catastrophic failure of pasture, and the Chase Syndicate had dudded itself again. In Humpty Doo there was too much water, at Esperance not enough.

The development was always controversial in the days before such infusions of foreign capital had become commonplace. Art Linkletter (who still has properties near Esperance) wrote in his book *Linkletter Down Under* that some Australians thought making land available to Americans was cheating the birthright of Australians. This was echoed in the *Bulletin* by David Frith, who said: 'It is regrettable Australians were never given a look in on the ground floor. It could have been financed with Australian capital.'

But although burned, the Americans stayed in there. In 1960 a group of American and Australian pastoral companies joined with the Western Australian government to establish the Esperance Land Development and open up the area for farming. Properties like 'Orleans Farms', and 'Link-letters Place' are reminders of continuing American involvement. In any case, Esperance eventually got its prosperous pastoral industry and still has it. The local penchant for triumphing over adversity is enshrined in the story of a pedigree local bull, which quaffed enthusiastically from a bath of sheep dip and drank itself dead. But so much of his semen had already been harvested that the deceased stud was able to continue contributing his noble genes to offspring for many years afterwards.

On a whim, Ros and I stopped by the Esperance Municipal Museum, near the Esplanade. It used to be a railway goods shed and houses a wonderfully eclectic collection ranging from a fully restored W919 steam engine (and wooden carriages), to farm machinery, antiques, and a splendid array of historical photographs. In pride of place are bits of Skylab, the orbiting space station which—continuing the connection between the region and spectacular American disasters—fell to earth near Esperance in July 1979 in a spectacular blaze of cosmic fireworks and world publicity.

When Western Australia looked the most likely target for Skylab, NASA tried to play down any threat to life and limb from the out-of-control space station, saying that it didn't matter if it fell in outback Australia as there were only kangaroos there anyway. The NASA flight control technicians made sure it didn't hit North America by making it tumble in space. On Thursday 12 July residents of remote stations in the Balladonia area reported being woken by the sonic boom and vibration of the man-made meteor hitting the district. It was later worked out that only 1.2 seconds in the timing of NASA's tumbling manoeuvre prevented Skylab landing plumb on the small railway town of Rawlinna. NASA offered $98 000 for a piece of Skylab, and a Hong Kong newspaper weighed in with an offer of an ounce of gold (then $259) for each ounce of debris.

The biggest chunk was found by midday on that Thursday, south of Rawlinna, by a Telecom technician, Bill Norton. It can be seen in all its splendour in the Esperance Municipal Museum today. It is about a metre in diameter, and two metres long, and appears to be coated with a substance similar to fibreglass. It had bounced and rolled on landing. Offers of riches began pouring into Noodoonia Station, which, station manager John Seller believed, must be littered with Skylab debris. A Perth tourist agency offered to fly him to the US if he took a bit of Skylab with him.

President Carter, no less, rang the mayor of Rawlinna to apologise on behalf of the United States government for the near miss. The mayor, according to press reports of the day, was a bit bemused by this.

Balladonia (population 14) on the Eyre Highway had never seen anything like it. American reporters descended on the settlement and became tired and emotional with the locals and each other as they fought for the one public telephone box situated under a gum tree. Mobile phones were not around then and, if they had been, would have been hopelessly out of range. An enterprising American photographer, who happened to be in Perth for the Miss Universe contest, bundled Miss USA into an aircraft and flew her to Balladonia for a photo opportunity. She was spotted trying to fix her lipstick in a cloud of dust. Two hours later her picture was being transmitted to New York from the vital telephone kiosk.

The local drinkers took it all in their stride, with some amusement. As they lounged outside the pub they heard one frustrated Yank reporter shouting to his New York editor from the phone box, 'Communications are difficult—this is Endsville man!'

The Australian Prime Minister, Malcolm Fraser, lightheartedly offered to swap bits of Skylab for a bigger quota for Australian beef in the US.

Feeling touristy, we decided to take the circular drive past the Pink Lake and around the coast. The same winds that gave Admiral D'Entrecasteaux such a hard time still blow strongly and regularly. So dependable are they that Esperance is the site of the first commercial wind farm in Australia, at Ten Mile Lagoon. The white towers and slowly turning 16-metre-diameter blades peep up over the hills as you drive around the coast road, looking like something out of a sci-fi thriller. The wind farm has only been running since 1993 and is operated by Western Power. Esperance is not connected to the state grid, and was entirely dependent on diesel-powered generators.

In two years of operation the wind farm electricity project has saved approximately three million litres of diesel fuel, 8300 tonnes of carbon dioxide emissions and more than one million dollars in fuel costs. Obviously the stronger the wind, the more electricity can be generated, but if the wind dropped, so would the power. To make sure the district's supply stays constant, computers control the output from the wind turbines so that the wind farm is never contributing more than 40 per cent of Esperance's power needs. A radio link between the wind farm and the diesel power station lets operators take best advantage of the conditions, shutting down or switching on the turbines as needed. It is all splendidly clean and green and I think the three-bladed turbines on their white 22-metre high towers look quite attractive and futuristic.

At Ten Mile Lagoon itself we caught a glimpse of some sailboarders apparently attempting suicide in the great rolling swells coming in uninterrupted from Antarctica. I grabbed the binoculars and watched horrified as one young man attempting to sail out through the surf disappeared under an enormous wave and, as far as I could tell from afar, did not reappear. We drove to a lookout point overlooking the small beach from which five of these brave souls were risking their lives.

The Nobel laureate Patrick White once said he thought the young men who provided such spectacular visual entertainment to passers-by, by surfing up and down the coasts of Australia, should be paid a special allowance by the Federal government. Come to think of it, until the dole provisions were tightened in recent years, they were! Finally one of the five punched his sailboard through the swells, and leaning against the south-westerly wind, powered his way further out to sea. Then he spun around, and came back to pick his wave, pirouetted and spun in a 360° turn on the face of the breaking swell, and delivered himself and sailboard seemingly effortlessly back to the beach in a smother of foam. I broke into spontaneous applause.

The young man sitting next to me on a bench seat was amused. It turned out he was from Switzerland—admittedly not famous for its surf. Kurt had managed to master the art elsewhere around the exposed coasts of Europe. He conceded the North Sea was bloody cold, even with a wetsuit. But he was not game to risk his neck at Ten Mile Lagoon and was content to watch.

Tomorrow we will drive to Hopetoun for Christmas. Back at camp, after one of Ros's famous stir-fries with—happy days—fresh vegetables instead of tinned bamboo shoots, I felt at peace with the world. Until Ros left The Manor and then reappeared cussing in vigorous terms.

'It's those stupid computerised locks on the toilet-block door. It's dark, and the buttons are not only ridiculously small, but shiny. It is a conspiracy against anyone over 40. Even if I had my glasses on I couldn't see to punch in the code. It is absolutely absurd.'

That was how I was found crouching outside the women's toilets, in the dark, shining a torch on the computer lock, apparently trying to get in.

'Constable—I can explain everything . . .'

Well, it didn't quite come to that. But I did get a very strange look from a woman camper who seemed oddly disturbed by what I was doing. It was not the best moment in the world for Ros to disappear into the shadows.

seven

A Fiery Christmas

There was indeed room at the inn for Christmas Eve at the Hopetoun Caravan Park. It is only about 200 kilometres west of Esperance, and we left Highway One at Munglinup and ran along the coast on quite good dirt roads (stopping for lunch and a swim at Munglinup Beach which is confusingly nowhere near Munglinup town some 25 kilometres further inland). Our genial hosts Peter and Lyn showed us to an excellent camp site, just behind the sand dunes leading to the beach. We were able to back The Manor into a little arboreal tunnel under over-arching trees—which was just as well, because it was stinking hot with gusts of incandescent wind sweeping down from the interior. We are now sheltered from the sun. It is such a top spot we may stay an extra night or three. Not only that, there are fireplaces and we may use one. We have planned a camp oven roast dinner for Christmas night.

Hopetoun was named after Australia's first governor-general, and had its busiest days before 1911 as a port and railhead for pastoral and mining interests. Its 430-metre wooden jetty was replaced in 1984 with a rock and gravel groyne which doubles as breakwater, car park and fishing platform. A summer swimming raft had been moored in the protected water, with children splashing about with joy. There is a charming old pub overlooking the groyne and seafront, and we found it necessary to sample several piercingly cold ales there. The young Irish barmaid had startlingly green eyes which the next day unexpectedly changed colour to an iridescent blue. Ros explained to me gently that I wasn't losing it—contact lenses as a fashion statement these days are not uncommon.

We had time to begin exploring the eastern side of the Fitzgerald River National Park, and climbed up the slopes of East Mt Barren where Ros was delighted to find some splendid specimens of *Barrens regelia*, a bright red wildflower unique to the area and a splendid view of the park and coastline to help us plan further exploration. Some walking tracks were closed, alas, because of the scourge of die-back, and we carefully brushed our boots before and after walking up the East Mt Barren track. The Fitzgerald River National Park is a fairly recent addition to the Western Australian list of national parks, and is controlled by the omnipresent Department of Conservation and Land Management.

CALM controls timber resources and state forests as well as conservation areas like national parks—responsibilities which sometimes sit uneasily together. Cynics have suggested (God forbid) that the only reason the Fitzgerald River National Park got up with CALM was that it didn't have any trees worth cutting down anyway. Today, both geologists and botanists rejoice in its diversity, because the coast was once connected to Antarctica before the great jigsaw of Gondwanaland drifted apart. (I was fascinated to find out that Hopetoun was once close to what is now Australia's Casey Station on the coast of Greater Antarctica.) UNESCO has listed the Fitzgerald National Park as an international biosphere reserve, one of only two in Western Australia.

On our way back to Hopetoun we met the park ranger, Mark, who was very worried about the prospect of bushfires. The weather was hot, and dry thunderstorms were forecast—with the possibility of lightning strikes. He told us the park was just recovering from being burnt out by lightning eight years ago. As things turned out, he was right to be so apprehensive.

The camping ground is filling up with families who come to Hopetoun especially for Christmas. The group opposite have been coming to the same spot for the last eleven years. Their caravan is fringed with Christmas decorations and flashing lights strung out into the trees near their camp. A fully decorated Christmas tree with baubles and rampant Santa has been positioned under the canvas of their annexe roof. Excited children from teenagers to ankle-biters are tearing about, trekking to and from the beach and checking out their favourite hide-aways from previous years doubtless recalling teen and sub-teen rites of passage.

One of those massive mobile holiday homes has moved in next to us. Brian is English, Caroline Australian. They have no children and Ros and I have conjectured that they are escaping from their respective family situations for Christmas. We have absolutely no evidence for this scurrilous theory. With the luxury of a fireplace (and some mallee roots) Ros rustled up a damper and I baked it in the camp oven. Brian asked to use the fireplace afterwards, which was just as well, because he had no axe and his quaint British theory of lighting a fire was to pile in some paper and put heavy logs on top. My still smouldering mallee roots saved the day.

We asked Brian and Caroline if we could have a look inside their hired mobile home. The interior was completely dominated by the bathroom and toilet, which had full head room, thus compressing the available living space so that kitchen, living space and bed were all squeezed in around the dunny. The necessary on-board collection tanks for shower water and other unmentionables led to an omnipresent smell of disinfectant in the van. That seemed a terrible price to pay for the luxury of an on-board pee in the middle of the night when there are perfectly clean and adequate toilet blocks in caravan parks and most camping grounds—or the good old-fashioned shovel and the stars above for bush camping. Brian said the hire company told them they weren't allowed to take the cumbersome van off the bitumen.

A cheerful extended Italian family has taken up residence on the bank behind us, and the mother of a bevy of teenage boys came down to ask if she could borrow 'an eggs'.

'Only one?' I asked her.

'Yes please.'

'Surely you will need more than one.' I called out to Ros. 'How many eggs do we have?'

She was adamant and became agitated. 'Only one eggs please. Only one.'

She strode to the fireplace and picked up our axe. 'Just one eggs. May I borrow please?'

Our axe became the 'eggs' for the rest of the trip.

As we were to cook a roast chook in our camp oven the next night, we indulged ourselves with a Christmas Eve dinner at the Hopetoun pub. Besides, I needed to check on the latest colour of the barmaid's eyes which were back from blue to green again. The pub surpassed itself with an excellent rare porterhouse steak, and a bottle of Merlot-Cabernet-Savignon for nine bucks. Unfortunately we did not sleep the sleep of the well-fed and the just because a cabin full of young Japanese students babbled and shouted until well past 2.30 on Christmas morning. It was so intrusive that I planned to get up at 6 am and sing Christmas carols loudly under their window. They thwarted me by departing in a bus—noisily—at 5 am.

Christmas morning dawned relatively cool and overcast, and the camping ground was really remarkably sedate save for the darting about of young persons on bright new bicycles with flashing iridescent discs and spanking paintwork. We decided to head into the Fitzgerald River National Park for a day of four-wheel-driving to Quoin Head. The Overland Telegraph used to pass close by but that track is now closed to help prevent the spread of die-back, and varied from soft sand (sometimes trenched deep below ground level) which Penelope handled with her usual aplomb. There is a camping area at Quoin Head, but only for tents from four-wheel-drive vehicles. The area has two splendid rocky headlands with a beautiful sandy cove. As we got close we could see the track ahead disappear over one of the headlands. I wondered idly where it went to, and then found out—straight down the bluff at what looked like a suicidal angle towards the camping ground. As others had obviously managed it, I gulped, engaged first gear in four-wheel drive and low reduction, and kept my foot clear of the brakes, like the book says, as Penelope 'walked' her way down at a sedate crawl.

Mark the ranger had told us to keep a lookout for flotsam and jetsam on the beach there. He said there was a warm current that swept around the coast at this time of the year, bringing in debris from a mini Sargasso Sea of seaweed some hundreds of kilometres to the west. Even the ubiquitous plastic bottles, he said, would be fringed with shellfish and marine life—and they were. We saw that kids had found some of them and put them in a tidal pool. Two white plastic detergent bottles were entirely surrounded with molluscs, poking out their feathery tendrils frantically as two large crabs took advantage of an unexpected meal.

We lunched at one of CALM's standard picnic tables. They even provide a free gas barbecue at a remote spot like this, although we did not use it. There were several families camping at Quoin Head and we thought of them two days later when savage bushfires forced them to leave. We had no way of knowing that the delightful coastal bushland we were enjoying was about to be devastated.

Because of our camp oven Christmas dinner, we made sure we were back to Hopetoun by 4 pm. The wind was blowing straight in the front of the fireplace, but our roast chook and vegies survived. We had carried with us from Sydney a vintage bottle of Bollinger, given to me by friends for my sixtieth birthday, and it seemed a good time to broach it. For the first time in my life I fired a champagne cork into the air which did not come down—

caught in the foliage above our camp. Some kind of omen? We accompanied the champagne with some Tasmanian smoked salmon. Camping, as previously mentioned, is not always about deprivation.

Our neighbours Brian and Caroline emerged from their elaborately packaged mobile dunny to share our fire, and join us for dessert. Caroline managed to rustle up Christmas pudding and custard, and we responded with Drambuie liqueur and Christmas cake complete with almond icing and those little silver bobbles, given to us by friends in Sydney for this moment. By 10 pm there seemed little wrong with the world or the universe.

We even managed to get up at 6 am on Boxing Day, and were away by 8 am. Our plan was to drive to the western side of the Fitzgerald River National Park, but around the top, not through the centre. Apart from the fact that the narrow roads are not recommended for caravans or trailers, there is a danger at holiday time of hooning four-wheel-drive enthusiasts collecting other travellers on blind bends.

Although the weather near the coast is comparatively dry and cool in midsummer—with temperatures around 26° Celsius or so—it is easy to become complacent about the extremes the Australian continent can turn on. Running along the South Coast road I became drowsy and suggested to Ros that we changed drivers. I opened the driver's door and stepped out of the airconditioning into the hot breath of hell. We had no idea, cocooned in the comfort of the Landcruiser, that the outside temperature had been boosted to around 42° by hot winds coming down from the interior. It was like being blasted by a blowtorch, and shook me up a bit. Although we had plenty of water and good equipment it was a sudden realisation of how unforgiving the Australian outback can be.

Turning south, and into the western side of the Fitzgerald River National Park—and noting a welcome drop in ambient temperature—we took a diversion down a four-wheel-drive track for 20 kilometres to a place intriguingly called Twertup.

Visitors to Western Australia are always fascinated by the number of towns and places ending in 'up'. The glib explanation is of an Aboriginal term meaning something like 'a meeting place where you will find water'. It ain't necessarily so. The 'up' part of the name simply means 'the place of', so the first part of the name is the important information. Cowaramup, for example, means the place of a small parrot. Yallingup is said to mean 'place of love', and 'Dwertup' was mentioned by the explorer John Forrest who came to the area in 1870. The Aboriginal name Dwertup refers to the dingo, but not necessarily to water. In fact, Forrest wrote of his camp there 'on a small branch of the Fitzgerald river near some granite rocks called Dwertup. At this spot there was water, but very little feed for the horses.'

The furphy about 'up' meaning water probably came about because Aboriginal names usually refer to old meeting places where fresh water is often found nearby. I hesitate to get into this debate, but that's what I believe to be the right story about all the 'ups'.

We were heading further into funny names territory, bound for the Horrie and Dorrie Walk, near their spongolite quarry at Twertup. Horace and Doreen Worth lived in the area between 1967 and 1973, cutting spongolite blocks from cliffs using a circular saw. In fact they built their house of spongolite, and it has now become the Twertup Field Studies Centre in the national park.

I had never heard of spongolite, which was formed somewhere between 45 and 50 million years ago after the Australian continent severed its last links with Antarctica. A shallow sea formed in which sponge organisms flourished in the warm water. Their lightly compacted skeletal remains sank into a sediment for Horrie and Dorrie to harvest aeons later from the eroded cliffs at Twertup. A light, soft, rather chalky stone, with occasional horizontal layers of clay or mud to give it texture, easily worked, and it has the excellent insulation qualities of a rammed-earth wall, but is far more elegant. The quarry, cut into the spongolite cliffs, looks like some ancient Mayan ruin, because the weather has rounded off the sharp edges where Horrie and Dorrie's circular saws once gouged out the soft blocks.

We parked Penelope and The Manor and pushed open the door of the late Horrie and Dorrie's happy home. Walking through the kitchen in the cool gloom created by the spongolite walls (which make a lovely interior feature), we were startled to see a couple sitting quietly in Horrie and Dorrie's armchairs in front of the fireplace in the lounge room. A couple of holidaying bird-watchers from Perth, had just done the nature walk nearby, and were enjoying the ambience of the house, while browsing through photo albums left by previous researchers and visitors. They said the walk was good value, with well-labelled flora (I could see Ros twitching with eagerness) and helpful historical information on signboards.

The walk finished up in the quarry, and was quite delightful. Driving out I spotted a magnificent Royal

Hakea with a yellow top, and rich red under-leaves. It seemed to glow with an internal fire, but these plants are notoriously difficult to photograph. As this one was in full sun, Ros was optimistic about a good image.

We got to Point Anne (which has a wonderful outlook over to Mid Mount Barren in the centre of the Fitzgerald River National Park) in time for a late lunch. The camp sites are not big enough for camping trailers but we found a 'group camping area', which fitted us nicely, behind some bushes which were a welcome buffer from the ferocious sea breeze, and hoped the park ranger would look kindly upon us. (We never saw him.)

Point Anne has a pit toilet but no showers, so we hurled our bodies into a surprisingly warm surf despite the cool wind, and vegetated happily in The Manor.

We woke next morning to the crack and rumble of thunder, and flashes of lightning. A corrugated-iron long drop is not a good place to linger in an electrical storm, so our essential visits were nervous and hurried. There were dramatic storm clouds and flurries of rain out to sea but, as Mark the ranger had feared, it was largely a dry storm—the worst possible scenario for the tinder-dry Fitzgerald River National Park.

I actually saw the lightning strike on the upper flanks of Mid Mount Barren which started one of the fires. Within a few seconds a wisp of smoke could be seen, followed by an obscene orange ring of fire which widened as we watched. Further to the east, there were smaller plumes of smoke also kindled by lightning strikes. Although we did not know it then, the eastern side of the park had been fired as well, and the campers we saw at Quoin Head were already being alerted to evacuate the area by park rangers.

By the time we finished breakfast, Mid Mount Barren was starting to look like a volcano, with a great plume of smoke streaming out to sea from its peak, and angry bars of flame sweeping up its flanks. It was fascinating but horrible to watch.

Two young English couples are camping nearby from a rented Toyota four-wheel drive. They are all originally from the north of England, and drove down in one day from Perth. We knew this, because after breakfast one young man asked if he could borrow the ignition key of our car in case it might fit theirs! I said I thought Mr Toyota had probably thought that one through and made such an eventuality unlikely. What was the problem?

It turned out that while they were on the beach one of the girls had borrowed the key from him to get something from the vehicle, and when he thought about it again, the key was nowhere to be found. Fortunately she had neglected to lock the back door, so they were able at least to get into the vehicle.

'At the moment', he said, 'we're trying to bust the steering lock by wrenching the wheel from side to side'. I thought Mr Toyota had probably thought of that one too, and I was right. 'By the way, could we have some water?'

The four of them had come to this waterless area with just a couple of plastic bottles of spring water, which were now finished.

We joined in the search for the key, sifting beach sand where they thought they had been. But as Chris the driver had also gone bodysurfing way along the beach and could have had the key in his pocket, no one had high hopes. So what to do?

The nearest town of any size, Bremer Bay to the west,

was 100 kilometres away. I noticed on my map that Quaalup Station, some 40 kilometres inland, advertised itself as a tourist destination. I offered to drive Chris there to make a phone call or two. Perhaps Quaalup stood for 'place of succour for silly Pommies'?

English people in Australia are often spooked by snakes and spiders, so it was appropriate that I ran over the only brown snake I saw on the road during our entire trip. Dale O'Brien, the cheerful manageress of the small shop, caravan park and historic homestead museum at Quaalup, was not very optimistic about finding a mechanic.

'There's only one travelling mechanic at Bremer Bay and I think he's just taken his family to Albany for the holidays.'

But sometimes fortune favours the gormless, and Chris not only managed to contact the bush mechanic, but convinced him to drive to Point Anne on a Sunday. I drove Chris back—an 80 kilometre round trip—and his thanks were perfunctory. Meanwhile Ros had found an emergency water tank near a CALM whale-watching vantage point about two kilometres from our camp site and told the two young Englishwomen about it. They seemed puzzled why this might be significant information. We got sick of them, and with the mechanic allegedly on his way, decided to take off for a drive to Hamersley Inlet for something to do.

The track was rough, with tyre-gouging stones lurking amongst the deeply trenched wheel ruts. It took a couple of hours to drive in and Hamersley Inlet looked muddy and unattractive compared with the beaches at Point Anne. We were also distracted by the alarming sight of the rampaging fire on Mid Mount Barren which by this time looked even more like an erupting volcano. And we were getting closer to it. Only one family was camped at Hamersley Inlet, but they were about to have company. On the way out we passed at least six four-wheel drives heading in. Passing was difficult, and in so doing we learned they were refugees from the eastern side of the Fitzgerald River National Park forced out by the fires.

Point Anne seemed a haven of peace and rest by comparison. The gormless Pommy key-losers were gone, so the bush mechanic must have found them and drilled out the steering lock. The firm who hired them the Toyota won't be too impressed. It will be an expensive weekend for them, I should imagine.

We shared a CALM gas barbecue with a couple from Perth and their 12-year-old son Rory. His mother confided that they thought it was the last time he would want to come on a holiday with them by himself before the hormone fairy waved her magic wand and his adolescent interests shifted. Ros and I thought she was almost certainly right. Rory was aglow after having caught quite a respectable salmon off the rocks, fishing with his father. Memo to self: never shake hands with a 12-year-old or anyone else cleaning a sea salmon before barbecuing chicken. Not only did the chicken taste fishy, but my hands seemed to reek of pungent fish guts for 24 hours.

The news on the radio is bad. Hopetoun is threatened by fires, including outlying properties and a thousand sheep. The fire in the Fitzgerald River National Park is out of control and is being left to burn itself out. All this from a couple of dry lightning strikes. Are we leaving an unintentional trail of disaster behind us? Ros reminded me that Cyclone Tracy blew Darwin away only a few weeks after we left it in our Kombi in 1974, and when we got to Hobart a few weeks later a ship knocked out the centre span of the Hobart Bridge. We will have to be more careful.

The God of Camping sent down a miserable flurry of drizzle on us as we were packing up The Manor next morning—just enough to streak the red dust all over the canopy and make a frightful mess which we had to fold into the trailer to close the roof for travelling. The sun then shone for the rest of the day.

We called in at Quaalup to see its historic homestead which, having been vandalised for about twenty years from the mid-1960s, was restored by the owners before Gil and Dale O'Brien who have it now. They have furnished it with appropriate historical bric-a-brac, and the elegant dining room is available for hire for special pre-arranged occasions. Gil and Dale also gave us directions for a short cut to Bremer Bay, which we later found meant approaching the town by driving across a sandbar—information which, for some reason, they neglected to mention.

The weather was cool and overcast and we didn't see Bremer Bay at its best. Apart from a large supermarket and a collection of fairly ordinary shacks there didn't seem much else. The fishing must be the drawcard. We were, however, able to do essential things like refuelling and telephoning Patty and Russell Leighton at their property in sight of the Stirling Ranges, 100 kilometres north-east of Albany.

Ros first met Patty Leighton in 1995 while recording interviews for a book for the ABC, *Women of the Land*, to celebrate the second year of the ABC Rural Woman of the Year Award. Patty was a finalist in the first year, 1994, and

Ros had interviewed her in a fairly rushed trip to Western Australia. The two women found an accord that seemed to reach beyond the formal interviewing session and kept in touch. When the Leightons heard we were coming to Western Australia in a more leisurely way, they invited us to stay.

As we drove towards the property Ros recalled her first hectic visit.

'After I interviewed Patty I had to drive north-east to Narrogin. I didn't have a clue about this area, except that I would be driving on back roads. Russell asked what I was going to do about lunch. I said I'd pick up something on the way. "Not where you're going", he said, and made me a cut lunch.

'Of course there was absolutely nothing between the property and Narrogin but bush and paddocks for 300 kilometres.'

Russell and Patty first met in Tasmania in 1958. Russell was an English engineer who had come out to work with the Hydro-Electric Commission, and Patty was a teacher. They met through a shared love of bushwalking and, after they married, bought a small mixed farm near Snug, about 40 kilometres south from Hobart. Four years later, the Leightons heard on the ABC Country Hour about some land opportunities in Western Australia and applied for what were called conditional purchase blocks in the Cape Riche area, north-east of Albany.

They didn't really hold out much hope of succeeding as they had no capital other than modest equity in their farm at Snug which they had hoped eventually to own. But they were awarded a block, so Russell set off from Tasmania in 1963 with an old Caterpillar tractor on an Albion truck, and drove across the Nullarbor—then just an unsealed goat track. This was the first of many trips Russell made from Tasmania to the block until he moved there permanently in April 1965. That same year Patty and their four children (including a three-month-old baby). She drove from Melbourne to Port Augusta in 150-kilometre stages, with her Mum helping with the kids, and on by train to Kalgoorlie. There Russell drove them in the Albion truck to a tent pitched in the wild, mallee-scrub country that he was attempting to clear for pasture.

In February 1966, with their eldest daughter Penny (6) due to start school, Patty and the children moved in to a half-finished corrugated-iron shearing shed, with the concrete still wet on the floor. They were not long settled in when Patty became pregnant with their fifth child—and they were still living in the shed twenty years later!

'So they have only had a proper house for the last ten or so years', I said to Ros as we drove in the gates of the property.

'Wait till you see it. It's not really a house, more a delightful living area, combining kitchen, living and dining room, that Patty built herself from spongolite blocks. As the kids grew up they built their own free-standing spongolite bedrooms where they wanted to, and where they could also go when they wanted some privacy. Patty and Russell did the same when they eventually moved out of the shed. So it's an unusual and quite charming little settlement.'

And so it was. We drove through the property gates into open paddocks, until we could see what amounted to a little settlement, crafted with the easily-worked chalky spongolite blocks that we had first seen at Horrie and

Dorrie's quarry in the Fitzgerald River National Park. Over the years, large eucalypts have grown up, shading the bungalow and outbuildings. I could see why Ros had been so enchanted with it all on her first visit.

Patty greeted us with a welcome cuppa and Russell came in for a break from repairing a recalcitrant water pump on a windmill-powered bore. Both of them are bursting with energy. Although Russell is in his early seventies, he is super-fit, whipcord thin, and planning ahead for the next ten years. Patty, equally fit, helps run the property, is heavily involved with regional land conservation, and has helped to write books not only on local history, but identifying some of the flora and fauna in the Cape Riche area near the coast.

Russell was pleased to see us for another reason. During the last three years the Leightons have taken the bold step of moving from sheep farming to growing Tasmanian blue gums. The project is partly financed by Japanese interests and, if all goes well, will result in the hardwood plantations being harvested for woodchips in seven years time. To keep track of growth rates, Russell has to measure groves of sample trees every few months—an elaborate procedure involving fitting together telescopic rods and raising them to the crown of the trees. Visitors are pressed into service. Within minutes we were bouncing through the paddocks in the beaten-up farm Toyota ute towards the acres of young blue gums, planted only a few metres apart.

The farm is on an ancient flood plain, with a tough layer of ironstone only a few centimetres beneath the ground so impenetrable that the roots of the large trees near the bungalow run along the ground in great twisted clusters, unable to get through. To grow a hardwood plantation—the Tasmanian blue gums have been genetically engineered to flourish in this area of marginal rainfall—a furrow is ripped through the ironstone, and the young trees then have to fend for themselves without extra water, while their tap roots get down into the damp clay subsoil.

To measure the trees I did the donkey work with the connected rods, Russell judged whether I was parallel with the treetops, and Ros did the maths. It was surprisingly hard work, and difficult to comprehend how Russell can do it by himself—which he said he mostly has to do.

Both Patty and Russell are pleased to be reforesting the land they cleared so completely thirty years before. At the time clearing all the mallee scrub seemed the only thing to do. Like the mallee country near Esperance, the soil only needed the right trace elements to have clover and pasture leap up so fast you could see it grow. Of course there were good and bad years, and insect pests did eventually move in. Now a mix of timber and pasture is known to be more friendly to the environment.

On our way back to the homestead we saw that Patty had found a dead sheep by the fence line. Ros went over to see if she could lend a hand and Russell asked me if I would like to see the property from the air. Minutes later he was wheeling a venerable Cessna 150 out of a corrugated-iron shed, and we were taxiing out to a grass strip which seemed rather close to a line of trees on the boundary. I noticed cobwebs on the instrument panel, but I also knew Russell was an experienced pilot. He had learned to fly with the Fleet Air Arm in Britain towards the end of World War II. In fact he had planned to make a career in civil aviation after the war, but was prevented from so doing by a severe stammer. So he switched to engineering and farming. His speech difficulties were no impediment to private flying, of course.

'Do you want a boring flight or an interesting flight?' he shouted over the engine noise as we prepared for take-off. In my youth, I once started flying lessons in Tasmania and went solo a couple of times before having to give up through lack of money and, it has to be admitted, my hopeless maths. That was shortly before my flying instructor was sacked for dangerous flying. He used to get bored doing circuits and bumps with rookies like me, and as we were using Chipmunk trainers in the 1950s (which were fully aerobatic and looked a bit like a scaled down World War II Spitfire) we would roar off high above the countryside to loop the loop and do a few spins and barrel rolls. I opted for an 'interesting' flight with Russell for old times' sake.

It was a glorious summer's day and as we gained height I was surprised at the extent of the blue-gum plantation now occupying about two-thirds of the property. Russell banked the Cessna steeply while I took a couple of photographs, and then gestured we would fly towards the coast and the Southern Ocean clearly visible about six kilometres to the south. As there were dual controls, I motioned to Russell that I wanted to see if I could still fly a plane forty years on. I managed to keep the Cessna on the straight and level, but was hopeless on turns, and very content to hand back control to the flying farmer.

We flew over the coast, and turned east towards Cape Riche. Russell decided to make the flight 'interesting' and we dropped down to just above wave height (although Russell assured me we never went below 500 feet) heading towards a small rocky offshore island, Haul Off Rock, where a colony of seals were sunning themselves between fishing excursions. I didn't see them at first, and Russell had fun with some steep turns doing several passes. He was also able to show me the camping ground at Cape Riche that we planned to visit in the next few days—and to entertain the Leightons. (Some of Russell and Patty's grandchildren were actually taking part in a swimming race as we flew over the sheltered bay, much to Russell's delight.)

Cape Riche was named after Admiral D'Entrecasteaux's botanist Claude Antoine Gaspard Riche, on a stormy night in 1792, and the area was settled in the early 1840s. Russell pointed out the stone homesteads of the first farms from the air as we headed back to the paddock airstrip among the flourishing Tasmanian blue gums.

Patty took me out to see the shed they had lived in for twenty years. Now used for storage, it was unchanged from the time they moved out into the spongolite 'homestead'. Earlier, she had told Ros:

> We put in some old carpets and built in a fireplace at one end, which invariably smoked so the whole shed was filled with smoke and we got a Metters No 1 stove up the other end and an old sink. We then moved to Tilley lanterns, which were hissing, very bright ones, and that was a move up . . .
>
> Eventually the power came in and that was just miraculous! We originally had the kerosene fridges but they also smoked, and they would either freeze everything or defrost everything; there never seems to be a happy medium and they were a real problem . . .
>
> In those days the mail was dropped in once a week and now it's three days a week, which is quite amazing. We had a wonderful old mailman; he used to pop the odd jelly bean in the mailbox for the

> children, and we'd get bread delivered out once a week from Albany.

The nearest doctor was over 100 kilometres away in Albany. Patty would ring him and give him the symptoms of a child's illness, and he'd ask what was in the medicine cupboard. If he was in doubt, he'd ask them to bring the patient in to Albany.

But by 1970 drought and falling wool prices forced the Leightons off their property and into a rented house in Perth. Russell went back to engineering, and worked on the farm at weekends. Patty got a job as a remote-area adviser for early childhood education. In 1978 Patty had to decide whether to go back to the farm or not. All her children were then either at university or school in Perth. The youngest, Kylie, was in Year Seven. Patty made the difficult decision to return to the farm and leave her children to fend for themselves in their house at Cottesloe.

> I really shudder when I think back to it. I feel somewhat deeply troubled that I left Kylie at such a young age, but they'd always been resourceful, and it worked. We had problems and the phone ran hot many a time, and we had interviews with headmasters over odds and ends, but the school knew what was happening, they knew the background, and we had made it quite clear that if there was a major problem we would be on the spot in very quick time.

To this day, Patty admits that was one of the hardest decisions she ever made, and still worries whether it was the right one. Then, after the children left school, each of them came back for a year on the farm and the spongolite stone-walled bedrooms began to proliferate. (Although spongolite is soft stone and easily cut, it is porous and had to be soaked in a diluted adhesive to enable the mortar to bond with it.) Patty and Russell were the last to leave the shed. And when Patty built the spongolite block walls to make the family living area, 'Russell thought it was a huge joke and he pretty well ignored it until it got to the roof stage'. When Patty said it was ready for a roof and said it was time Russell did something about it, some of the angles were rather odd.

> He'd bought all this old timber from structures that they'd knocked down in Albany, so none of the timber he was working with was straight—a lot of old karri and jarrah full of notches and things—so he not only had to fit it on to my crooked structure, he also had to fit in this crooked timber. But it sits there and it's proved to be a great venue.

Patty also made a dining-room table and chairs from heavy jarrah planks.

Leaving the Leightons' farm was made slightly less painful by the knowledge we would be entertaining them to lunch in a day or so. It was only a short run down to Cape Riche, and we picked up some bait and fuel at the Wellstead Store on the way. We have not entirely abandoned the hope of catching some fish with our elaborate beach rods.

The Cape Riche camping area is not run by CALM but by the local community and council, and is old-style Aussie camping which has all but disappeared from the east coast. Long-term residents were comfortably established with great piles of firewood beside their fireplaces, and the couple near us had—horror of horrors—a generator! But it was a relatively quiet one, and they only ran it during the daytime. We were lucky not to be near one at the top of the site which sounded like a DC3 warming up. The camping ground is on a small promontory with a sheltered beach—the same beach from which Russell and I had seen from the air his grandchildren busily swimming out to a moored raft. There is a fairly eclectic mix of people here. The campers to the south of us have a large fishing boat on a trailer regrettably named *Screamin' Semen*. On their truck is the proudly emblazoned legend: 'Shit doesn't happen, arseholes cause it.'

On the seaward side, close to where we have positioned The Manor, there is an interesting looking old stone building which we discovered was the original storage shed set up by one George Cheyne, who migrated from Scotland in 1831. Cheyne (then in his forties) was unable to get any land on the Swan River, moved to King George Sound and eventually to Cape Riche in 1839. There he presided over an unofficial settlement where foreign and local whaling ships anchored to avoid port dues at Albany. Cheyne traded tea, sugar, rum and dungaree cloth for sandalwood, fresh vegetables, meat, butter and fuel. When farming got under way in the 1840s, the wool was manhandled in open boats through the surf to coastal schooners.

Without high hopes, Ros and I took our rods and expensive bait down to the shore, and donated it to tiddlers which expertly removed it without being caught. Perhaps it was just as well, as we would have had to throw them back. It is just as well we have a curry scheduled for tonight. Tomorrow, the Leightons are coming for lunch. We will try again in the morning.

*

A stiff onshore breeze has stymied fishing and also provided some early-morning drama. As I headed out to inspect the beach, a rather dazed elderly gent half-staggered past. When I asked if he was OK he said he needed a stiff drink. 'Bit early in the morning isn't it?'

'Not when you've just had a tree fall on you, mate.'

The old bloke had been sleeping in a canvas caravan annexe, when without warning an old leaning gum, partly eaten out by white ants, suddenly fell on the caravan. Fortunately a big branch caught on the side of the caravan and the annexe did not get the full impact, but it was a near thing. George, the camp caretaker, and one of the *Screamin' Semen* crew were already at work with a chainsaw. It looked worse than it was. When they pulled the rest of the tree away, the caravan was not damaged, the canvas of the awning wasn't even ripped, and the only casualties were a smashed polystyrene beer cooler and a bent awning support pole. The old chap went home later that day, still badly shaken. The wind change had obviously been the final straw for the weakened tree.

I took a few photos and promised to send a print to the owners. George the caretaker said that some little boys had been sleeping in a flimsy tent in that same spot only a week before, so things could have been far worse.

The Leightons arrived at noon, as arranged, for a pre-lunch swim. Russell, being Russell, did not swim from the beach but walked out to the point, dived in off the rocks, and swam around the long way to the swimming raft. During lunch he asked me if I was fit. I said I thought I was reasonably fit for a man of my age. He received this intelligence inscrutably and did not comment.

After lunch Russell suggested we walk to Cape Riche—the spot we had seen from the air. Ros and I both like walking and the trek to the cape took about an hour. The view was superb, and a modest swell crashed in on the cliffs from the Southern Ocean. Russell (who at 71 is eleven years older than me) was leaping about like a mountain goat, teetering on the top of sheer cliffs, and scrambling up large boulders to get a better view. Then I found out why he had inquired about my fitness.

'Tim and I will walk back around the rocks', he said firmly. Ros and Patty headed off along the headland the way we had come, and I looked wistfully at the established track. Russell was already down at the shoreline, bouncing along on his thin brown legs with the agility of a 12 year old. I used to like hopping around shoreline rocks when I was that age, and haven't done much of it since. It was all I could do to keep him in sight, although he kindly paused from time to time to let me catch up. Only sheer adrenalin and fear of the humiliation of a helicopter rescue if I broke a leg kept me going. Russell seemed totally unruffled and imbued with inhuman endurance. As the Leightons headed back to their farm, I knew I'd be stiff for a week. The only consolation for my injured pride and muscles was that Russell would not know that. Or perhaps he did . . .

It is time to change our plans again. We will not go to Albany—our next scheduled destination—tomorrow, but head north-west and inland through Mt Barker and up to the Margaret River area and explore the coastline (and sample the product of some of the legendary vineyards there), before heading down through the timber country back to Albany. Sadly, after that, we will be heading home rather more quickly than our discursive journey west. But we will not think of that yet.

The camp was unusually quiet for our last night at Cape Riche, partly because the *Screamin' Semen* brigade had left. We managed an early start, and arrived in Mt Barker by 9 am. Ros was keen to visit the *Banksia* farm there, and I had designs on the Plantagenet Winery. A *Banksia* farm—is this an unknown Australian niche primary industry? Farewell emu farms, it's time for the annual *Banksia* harvest . . . Not so, said Ros. 'It just so happens that there is a bloke here who has managed to grow every variety of *Banksia* that exists in Australia and I want to go there.'

Now I am not one to deny individuals their grand passions, whatever they may be. Kevin Collins, the 'Banksia Man', even looks like one. His genial bearded visage under his brown bush hat could almost have come straight from a May Gibbs illustration. He and his wife Cathy are building a wonderful house of local stone, and are remarkably welcoming to occasional blow-ins like Ros and me, as well as larger, organised tours.

Their extensive garden has 76 varieties of *Banksia* (plus some hybrids) and spectacular natives like *Dryandra*, *Hakea*, kangaroo-paws and other unique Western Australian flora. The riskiest part of opening up the garden to visitors is that someone might tramp in with the dreaded die-back fungus *Phytophthora*. To guard against that, Kevin insists all visitors first stand briefly in a shallow tray of chlorine, so concentrated I half-expected to leave the soles of my sneakers behind as I stepped out.

As we admired the incredible variety of *Banksias*, Kevin recalled the proud moment when Australia's number one *Banksia* expert came to confirm the scope of his collection. 'Yep, you've got 'em all, Kevin', said the botanist. 'Some are incorrectly labelled, but you've got the lot.'

After our tour, Kevin invited us into a display room dedicated to *Banksia* memorabilia. Some of the larger cones of *Banksia grandis* look like echidnas, with brown furry noses. There are *Banksia* cones turned in a lathe as vases, wine goblets and eggcups. I may even have seen a *Banksia* honey-twirler, but I can't swear to it. We bought a *Banksia* egg to go with our collection of ceramic and stone eggs in Sydney.

Ros and Kevin launched into a frenzy of Latin botanical names, and Ros promised to send him seeds from a *Banksia serrata* that grows near our beach house on the east coast—which he had of course, but a smaller tree than he was used to. It was a touching moment.

It was as well we had gone to the *Banksia* farm first, as it was late morning and almost a respectable tasting time when we pulled in to the Plantagenet Winery, one of several noted vineyards in the district. I thought this was a rather pretentious name, but found to my shame that it merely reflected the Shire of Plantagenet. No one seems to know why Governor Stirling, the instigator of the original Western Australian settlement, so grandiloquently named the shire. Some bottles of pinot noir, riesling, and champagne (I know we are not supposed to call it that) found their way into Penelope's wine cellar.

A little further north, Ros handed me a cup of coffee while I was driving—not an unusual happening—but on this occasion I managed to fumble the handle and hurl most of it into my crotch. Fortunately it was not at boiling point, but still painful. My temper was not improved. I pulled over, cussing and swearing, knowing that only a complete change of shorts and underwear could remedy the situation. While I fulminated and rummaged for fresh clothes Ros walked back towards a small trailer advertising fresh apricots.

She came back with a great mountain of apricots in a carton.

'Why on earth did you get all those?' sez I, still grumpy. 'We can't possibly get through all that.'

Ros said there was nothing she could do about it. She asked for a kilo at the advertised price, but the seller kept on piling the apricots in.

'When I said to him that he was giving me too many, he said they were his apricots so he could do what he liked with them!'

eight

Rolls-Royce Chardonnay at a BMW Price

We are taking a slightly circuitous route to Margaret River, up the Albany Highway to Kojonup, then turning north-west to Collie and on to Bunbury before turning south again, down the coast road through Busselton to the Margaret River region which sticks out into the Indian Ocean like the flank of a pork chop, with Cape Leeuwin (and its lighthouse) on its southern extremity, and Cape Naturaliste (also with lighthouse) to the north.

Memories are triggered as we head up the Albany Highway. I have been here before—so long ago that it doesn't bear thinking about. All right, I'll confess. It was 1959, nearly forty years ago. At that stage I was the motoring editor of the Hobart *Mercury*, aged all of 22, covering the Vacuum Oil Company's Mobilgas Economy Run, which began in Perth and for the next three days took in Albany, Busselton and Bunbury, and then looped west to York (to the east of Perth), up to Goomalling and Toodyay and back to Perth by the Great Eastern Highway. Being a Tasmanian in a Perth pub in 1959 represented travel exotic enough to have perfect strangers buy me a beer on the strength of it.

I can't recall why the Vacuum Oil Company started their economy runs, because it was well before any oil crises or talk of fossil-fuel resources running out. Just a smart idea by an adman I expect. Some drivers drove barefoot to depress more delicately their accelerator pedals and regulate the flow of petrol through leanly adjusted carburettors. The road surfaces varied from good bitumen to rough, rutted gravel. The motoring press were very well cared for. Before we left Perth we were ushered into a basement cellar and asked to strip to the waist before launching ourselves at newspaper-covered trestle tables groaning with fresh crabs, washed down with Swan lager, of course.

It was all very blokey although one all-woman crew (they were 'girls' in those days), Misses J Annear and J Johnson, crewed a Holden and were involved in the economy run's only serious accident on the second day when their car skidded in a sand patch and hit a tree. The young woman on the passenger side was thrown out (in those pre-seatbelt days) but not seriously hurt.

I remember being enormously impressed by the new technology which enabled a small refrigerator to be built into the boot of our press car: it held precisely nine cans of cold beer.

One bonus of being on the trip was meeting Jules Feldman, then editor of *Modern Motor* in Sydney, and developing a friendship which has lasted to this day. Jules had an interesting background. His parents were Russian and Jules had been born in Siberia and brought up in China. (He showed me how to use chopsticks during a 30-second lesson in a Perth Chinese restaurant for which I

(Left) It's true. Four-wheel-drive vehicles bog down on beaches if their tyres are too hard—even Toyota Landcruisers. Author having a necessary deflating experience on the beach at Thomas River, Cape Arid National Park. (Right) Our farmer friend Ken seemed to have a stubby holder permanently grafted to his hand—and an inexhaustible supply of cold tinnies in his truck. (Photograph, Greg Williams)

'Cocktails at Six', at Thomas River. From left: Heather Messer, Todd (8), Ryan (6), Greg Williams and Ros Bowden.

The blue and sheltered haven of Lucky Bay, Cape Le Grand National Park, named and visited by Matthew Flinders in 1802.

Author triumphant on the top of Frenchman's Peak, Cape Le Grand National Park.

(Left) A splendid specimen of Western Australian Royal Hakea whose leaves seem to burn with an inner fire. (Right) Not ancient Mayan ruins, but the remains of Horrie and Dorrie's spongolite quarry now part of the Fitzgerald River National Park.

Horrie and Dorrie's splendid spongolite-block house is now a field study centre for the Fitgerald River National Park.

Kevin Collins (the 'Banksia Man') has every known variety of Australian *Banksia* growing at his farm near Mt Barker—all 76 of them. Ros was entranced.

Unbelievably, no one was hurt when this tree fell on a caravan annexe at the Cape Riche camping ground. An elderly camper who was asleep inside it at the time had a tot of rum for breakfast to steady his nerves.

(Left) Originally logged a century ago, it has taken another 100 years for these magnificent karri trees to re-establish themselves in the Margaret River area. (Right) It was the sight of ten-year-olds scampering up the steel-spike ladder of the 61 metre-tall Gloucester Tree near Pemberton that caused the sexagenarian author to have a go himself.

Author cools his heels (and other parts) at Sue's Bridge, near Nannup.

Some unique Western Australian flora: (top left) *Banksia speciosa*; (top right) Western Australia's state flower, the kangaroo paw—*Anigozanthos*; (bottom) blossom and distinctive horn-shaped buds of *Eucalyptus lehmannii*.

The Cape Leeuwin lighthouse—opened in 1896—marks the extreme south-west tip of the Australian continent, where the Southern and Indian Oceans meet.

It was difficult to avoid sampling Western Australian wines at innumerable, delightful small vineyards—some of which only sold their product at the cellar door. It seemed churlish to pass them by.

The whale chaser *Cheynes IV*—now high and dry at Albany's Whaleworld—is a stark reminder of the days when the world's great whales were almost hunted to extinction. Whaling stopped at Albany as late as 1978.

Ros, donating expensive bait, on the beach at Cape Riche. We didn't catch a decent feed the entire trip.

am still grateful. Few Australians knew how to use them in the 1950s.) It was Jules who drew my attention to a notice on the wall of our Bunbury guesthouse: DO NOT SQUASH MUSQUITORS ON WALL. As he later wrote in his *Modern Motor* report, 'Gory streaks on the whitewash wall showed tenants didn't take instructions seriously . . .'

The motoring press were rushed around to various sections of the route, taking short cuts to observe the passing parade while keeping the summer heat at bay with the occasional cold tinnie from the ingenious carboot fridge. As Jules rather unkindly (but with justification) wrote in his *Modern Motor* dispatch, 'when 200 men are thrown together for a few days, there's sure to be at least one earbasher':

> This year's was a beauty . . . travelled in a press car (but wasn't a pressman) . . . discoursed on everything in sight, knew everything . . . how many sheep to the acre around Brookton; what's the wheat yield farther south; how much milk a Jersey gives at Mt Barker; how to tell a karri tree from a jarrah . . . When companions started to doze off, he'd prod them awake: 'See, see! That's a jarrah! You could build six houses out of that one.' And when he ran out of conversation, he'd pull out a mouth-organ and wheeze away at that.

I remember him well. Although this fellow was a classic bore, he could not take the edge off a joyous three days. By the way as a matter of historical interest, the best fuel consumption achieved was by a Morris Minor at a smidgen under 50 miles per gallon. The cars were divided up into four classes depending on engine capacity and manual or automatic transmission, and the overall winners were a Citroen DS-19 (39.08 mpg), followed by a Peugot 403

(42.99 mpg), and a Wolseley 6/90 third (31.40 mpg).

Now, nearly forty years on, I was back towing a camping trailer and chewing up diesel with a six-cylinder engine at flow rates and fuel prices I didn't want to think about. We decided to eschew the delights of Bunbury and Busselton because our time was running out and press on down the coast to the Margaret River district of which we had heard splendid things, all of which turned out to be true. The area is more wooded than I had imagined, with the original dairy farms being converted gradually to vineyards.

We have booked ourself into Prevelly Park camping ground which is a bit out of town, but close to a number of beaches and quite near where the Margaret River estuary cuts inland from the sea. The spot we have been allocated is pleasant and shady, under a quintessentially Western Australian peppermint tree, up on a terrace at the rear of the park. Local lore has it that the summer season does not begin until the peppermint trees shed their flowers. When it does begin, the climate is wonderfully predictable. Summer days are clear and pleasant, with hardly any humidity and with sea breezes to bring relief on the hotter days. Margaret River rainfall is dictated by the 'Roaring Forties' which move north in the Australian winter and south in summer, matching the rotation of the earth. This conveniently unloads 85 per cent of the annual rainfall during the six months' winter season.

I described the Margaret River region between the two lighthouses, Leeuwin to the south and Cape Naturaliste to the north, as being like the meaty flank of a pork chop, standing out from the west coast. When the Gondwanaland split into its continental components, the district was briefly an island until the 10 000-metre-deep trough to the east filled up with sand as a result of prevailing winds and currents, and is now the world's largest and richest mineral sands deposit.

Over millions of years the granite 'island' has crumbled, and produced rich free-draining gravel soils which just happen to be the bee's knees for growing vines for premium-quality grapes. With oceans virtually on three sides, Margaret River has its own microclimate, frost free in winter and dependably fine in summer. It is uncannily similar to the Bordeaux region of France except that Margaret River has a longer dry, warm period to ripen the fruit. Whereas the poor old Bordeaux growers have a 'great' vintage every now and then, subject to the vagaries of the European summer, Margaret River has one every year!

None of this was realised until 30 years ago, when a few wine enthusiasts began planting out vineyards among the dairy farms, in the belief that they could produce outstanding wines. The pioneers were three medicos, Tom Cullity, Kevin Cullen and Bill Pannell, mining engineer John Hohnen, and a chartered accountant turned industrialist, Denis Horgan. The vineyards they established, Vasse Felix, Cullens, Moss Wood, Cape Mentelle and Leeuwin Estate are the blue bloods—and best known—of the profusion of later wineries which range from boutique to more substantial operations.

Although Margaret River only produces about one per cent of Australia's wine, its remarkable location, completely dependable climate, and the quality of the product have wine writers piling superlatives upon superlatives, while much of the market for the top-class Margaret River wines is now overseas. Fifteen years ago, farmland in the area was going for about $500 an acre. Today it's more like $5000 or even $10 000. Some of the hippies who bought land twenty or so years ago have done really well.

No wine in the Margaret River area is cheap. Fortunately for the traveller, some of the smaller vineyards sell only from their cellar doors, although it is hard to come by a bottle under $15. Some of the premium chardonnays are over $70 a bottle. The wine writer James Halliday has likened the predictable excellence of Leeuwin Estate's premium chardonnays to the white wine equivalent of Grange Hermitage—'Rolls-Royce Chardonnay at a BMW price', as he put it.

We have been given an introduction by some friends in Perth to Bob Cartwright, the winemaker at Leeuwin Estate, and hope he has time to see us. The distances are quite modest: it is only an 80-kilometre drive between the two lighthouses, and Prevelly Park where we are camped (and the Margaret River itself) is conveniently at the halfway point on the coast. The plan is to head south first to the Cape Leeuwin lighthouse, and then do some touristing before bearding Mr Cartwright in his den at the good tasting time of 4 pm. (We spoke by phone and he seems pleased to have us. We didn't need to be asked twice.)

The town of Margaret River is quite charming, but what was once a fairly basic Aussie farming service town has become increasingly trendified, with art galleries, souvenir shops and travel agents well represented. Determined to do some research before we set off the next day, we asked about the limestone caves with which the region is well-blessed. There are two alternatives. One is to pay your money at one or more of the commercially run caves, and go on a conducted tour. However, the ubiquitous CALM runs a number of the caves where you are encouraged to explore by yourself with a lamp and simple instructions, for a token fee. In the town of Margaret River, at the tourist bureau and travel agents, the CALM caves remain a closely guarded secret. In fact, I challenge any visitor to establish that they actually exist! There are no CALM pamphlets on display, just the commercial glossies. There is a conspiracy of commercial silence when you ask about the government-run caves. The closest we got to finding out was a muttered 'go to the CALM office and ask', and then our informant seemed to go deaf when we asked where that was.

I suppose we should have persevered, but it all got too hard. (Later we did meet one young mother who had managed to get the CALM information and found that one of their caves was very near a commercial operation but not at all well signposted. The commercial cave operators said it wasn't open. Her kids had a wonderful time exploring in their own time and away from the madding crowd with their hired flashlights.)

Next morning we decided to drive down the Caves Road (which is parallel with the faster Bussell Highway but closer to the coast) from which most of the forests, caves and other attractions can be accessed. An early delight was our first karri forest, unique to the south-west corner of Western Australia. These smooth-barked forest giants are actually regrowth from logging a century ago. It is like standing in a natural cathedral. The trunks are free from branches for 20 metres and more, as they thrust up towards the light and sun. It is quite remarkable that the karris have regenerated to such a size in just 100 years of regrowth.

Just looking at them—which I didn't get a chance to do during the hectic progress of the Mobilgas Economy Run—I almost forgave my earbashing companion in 1959. These trees are truly the aristocrats of eucalypts. Unfortunately the high-rainfall country in which they flourish is also prized dairy country so many stands were cleared for pasture in the early years. Their straight-grained wood, which dries to a deep purplish colour, is used for general construction and flooring. The rough-barked jarrah eucalypt is a less-spectacular tree, but its distinctive dark-red timber is more commercially prized. It was ideal for railway sleepers in the early years, and is today superb for furniture and craft as well as housing and construction. It, too, only grows in the south-west of Western Australia.

Of the many caves on offer, the Jewel Cave was the one we decided to sample on our way south to the Cape Leeuwin lighthouse. The tour took an hour and was, we thought, worth the unexpectedly steep entrance fee. The usual motley group of camera-toting tourists of all ages (including a noisy bevy of primary-school-aged children) were ushered into an air-lock that separates the atmosphere in the cave from the outside world. This is important to maintain the moisture levels and stillness of the air inside because, among its other treasures, the Jewel Cave has the world's longest straw stalactite hanging down from the ceiling not far from the entrance—a remarkable 5.9 metres. Jewel Cave is named after the many delicate filigree stalactites (and stalagmites) that have formed curious shapes like free-form modern jewellery.

Our Scandinavian guide, Annalese, was very well informed and cheerful—even with a clutch of rampaging ankle-biters testing her patience by whooping and hollering and running along the walkways. I saw one urchin about to leave the pathway and head off into forbidden territory (thereby trampling ancient stalagmites) and stopped this illegal excursion by transfixing him with such a ferocious look that it almost turned him into limestone. What his parents were doing at the time I knew and cared not.

The cave has the usual organ pipes and shapes resembling sculptures of various forms including a very realistic camel, although I noticed someone had enhanced the resemblance by adding an eye. Jewel Cave is also famous for the discovery of the fossil remains of a Tasmanian Tiger, dated at 25 000 BC. The tiger has gone, but there is the sad mummified skeleton of a poor little possum which must have fallen through a hole made by a tree root in the roof of the cave god knows how many hundred years ago, and wandered around hopelessly until lying down to die a lonely death in utter darkness in the lowest reaches of the cave.

Talking of total darkness, Annalese tried to organise that for us by switching off all the fixed cave lights. Unfortunately the red glow of various cameras and video recorders carried by our companions took away from the experience of being completely without any light in the velvety blackness.

Down in the lowest sections of the cave, it was clear that the water level had dropped in fairly recent times leaving discoloured black markings on the limestone. It was as if the tide had gone out. In a way it had. Annalese explained that when the great original karri forests above had been felled first for timber and to clear land for dairy farms, the watertable had risen. Ros later told me that just one big karri tree sucks up hundreds of litres of water every 24 hours and puts most of it out into the atmosphere through transpiration. The watertable has dropped again by at least a metre because of the regrowth over the last century, clearly marked on the limestone bordering the lowest reaches of the cave floor.

Back into the sunshine we headed Penelope towards Cape Leeuwin, believed to have been named by an early Dutch navigator in the ship *Leeuwin* in 1622. Unfortunately there is no hard historical evidence of the ship's visit, although the discovery of a seventeenth-century clog at nearby Flinders Bay in 1930 suggests that the master and crew of *Leeuwin* may have put in there for water.

Matthew Flinders did not name the bay after himself, that was not his style. It was named much later. Flinders, however, does give Cape Leeuwin a mention in his 1801 voyage in *Investigator*, recording in his log on 7 December: 'I nominate Cape Leeuwin, as being the south-western, and, most projecting part of Leeuwin's Land.'

It was certainly a suitable and necessary place for a lighthouse, and the one at Cape Leeuwin is a beauty, first opened in 1896. The original clockwork mechanism on top of its tall tower has been bypassed by electric motors, but it can still be seen, and the wonderful glass prism reflectors of the original light are still flashing its distinctive signature to mariners every night. The three original light-keepers' cottages are also well preserved. Cape Leeuwin is the most extreme south-west point of the Australian continent, where the Indian Ocean meets the Southern Ocean. As I have a considerable interest in Antarctic history, and now have crossed the Southern Ocean eight times in four visits to the Antarctic continent, I simply had to pose for a happy snap by the sign illustrating the meeting point of the two oceans.

In an adjoining bay we whipped our cameras out again to photograph a waterwheel and wooden flume that used to supply the lighthouse keepers' cottages from a nearby spring. The system was used until 1928 and the carbonates in the mineral-rich water have been slowly turning it into stone ever since. Today it is a fine and unusual sight, the big calcified wooden wheel dripping water over its mossy flanks.

Keeping in mind our wine-tasting and tour at Leeuwin Estate at 4 pm, we began heading north again, but were unable to resist checking out delightful little holiday hideaways like Hamlyn Bay, where school-holiday campers were fishing and swimming in crystal sheltered waters bordered by rocky headlands. It is just as well for the locals that it is all so far from the dreaded eastern states—these superb spots would be swamped by holiday-makers escaping the humidity and monsoony summer weather of New South Wales and Queensland. Perhaps there is something to be said for the tyranny of distance.

At 4 pm, tastebuds salivating gently in anticipation, we drove into the Leeuwin Estate, situated in its own rural valley, where the winery overlooks a natural amphitheatre with its own private karri forest as a backdrop. This amphitheatre is used on special occasions for opera and concert performances, and glittering occasions they have been, with audiences of up to 6500 enjoying artists of the calibre of Dame Kiri Te Kanawa, Ray Charles, Diana Ross, Dionne Warwick, Tom Jones and George Benson.

Leeuwin Estate makes its wine on the premises, and there are restaurant and bar areas where you can sample its product while enjoying the spectacular view across the valley. We asked for the winemaker Bob Cartwright, who was expecting us. 'As a matter of fact I have a surprise for you,' he said. 'Our chairman Denis Horgan is here and would like to meet you.'

Denis, a fit-looking 57-year-old with a passion for surfing, greeted us amiably and took us for a quick conducted tour around the winery, among great stainless-steel tanks ringed with frosted pipes, processing the latest vintage, while the harvest of yesteryears lay in great racks of French oak casks in airconditioned comfort.

The man who made it all, Bob Cartwright joined us on the terrace where Denis called for some samples of Leeuwin's finest joy juice. It has to be admitted that correct tasting procedures were not observed. With the top-of-the-range bottles selling overseas in excess of sixty bucks a bottle it would have been churlish to spit any of it out. (There was no bucket available anyway.) Swallowing seemed the way to go as we moved happily through the rieslings, chardonnays, sauvignon blancs and cab savs that Denis kept urging upon us.

Some of the finest grapes are kept for the 'Art Series' wine, each with a reproduction of a painting by a noted Australian artist on the label of every grape variety. Denis Horgan told us that Leeuwin has 42 acres of Chardonnay grapes, but the famous 'Block 20' not only is the origin of the Art Series wine, but produces the continuity of excellence that has caused wine writers like James Halliday to call it the white equivalent of Grange Hermitage. The vines on Block 20 are now 16 years old, with their roots deep in the well-drained granite gravel soil. Yields are moderate, never more than 2.5 tonnes to the acre, but the small bunches of grapes have enormous natural acidity and varietal flavour.

'Does each vine have its own pet name?' I asked Denis while burying my nose into the triumphant results of Block 20. 'Just about', he said cheerfully.

The Margaret River wine industry is very young. The first vineyards to be established in the late 1960s were Vasse Felix and Cullen. Denis had had a farm at Leeuwin since the 1960s, but in 1972 got a call from his Perth lawyer saying that a couple of overseas visitors were interested in buying the property.

'I asked him why the hell he was even asking me—he knew I loved the farm so much I'd never sell it. But I was intrigued and asked to meet them, even though I had no intention of selling.'

It was a fateful meeting.

One of the interested parties was the noted wine expert and connoisseur, Robert Mondavi, from California's Napa Valley. Mondavi told Horgan that he believed Margaret River's climate and soils were ideal for growing premium-quality grapes, that he had been looking around the area and Horgan's farm was the ideal location for such activity. Denis Horgan didn't sell him his farm, but began a cooperative relationship in which Mondavi was the mentor of the fledgling Leeuwin Estate and played a vital role in cloning vines, selecting the best growing sites, and advising on varietal characteristics. A nursery was planted in 1974 and the first trial vintage was in 1978. Horgan's friendship with Mondavi continues to this day.

The sun was setting over the distant karri trees when Bob Cartwright, the winemaker, took his leave. Denis cracked another bottle, which seemed a terrifically good idea at the time. He is one of those people who is interested in self-awareness and the maximising of personal opportunities, not only of himself, but of others. As the level in the latest bottle dropped in time with the sinking sun, he quizzed me about my plans for the future, and between us we devised wondrous schemes of business and personal fulfilment that had the potential to make me so much money I could barely climb over the pile of it to reach the door and say goodbye. Denis had an evening engagement (and clearly a tolerant life's partner awaiting his return) but it was after 6 pm before we all headed out to the car park.

I did not drive. It has to be admitted I have only a hazy memory of getting back to Prevelly Park.

The next day we decided to drive up to see the lighthouse marking the northern extremity of the Margaret River area, Cape Naturaliste. On the way up (still driving on Caves Road) we dropped into a place called Canal Rocks, and were glad we had. The 'canal' is a natural channel through a rocky promontory, over which a single log bridge had been erected but was not safe to use and had been closed. No matter, we sat down by the canal's edge and watched children snorkelling and swimming in the clear water, fringed with colourful kelp and seaweed. It looked so delightful I made a personal vow to take up underwater snorkelling again.

In comparison with the Cape Leeuwin light's splendid tower, the light at Cape Naturaliste is a modest structure only about fifteen metres tall. Unlike the Leeuwin light, you are not permitted inside unless you pay a fee for a guided tour. There is a most interesting maritime museum in one of the lighthouse keepers' cottages, but we decided not to take the tour of the light itself after the thrill of climbing the inner stairs of Leeuwin—for free.

Making our way south again, and on a whim, we turned into the Wise Winery and restaurant near the town of Dunsborough only a few kilometres from the Cape Naturaliste light. Perhaps we were spoiled by our Rolls Royce insider treatment at Leeuwin Estate, but I was disappointed at their tasting policy. They had a mean little measuring thing on the bottle that hardly stained the bottom of the glass with wine—you could barely taste it! So we headed to the coast for a swim and a picnic lunch at a beach near the town of Yallingup. It was so hot we waded out and stood up to our necks in the cool Indian Ocean with water so clear I could see portion-sized whiting darting about our feet without using my underwater mask.

Refreshed, we decided to try another small winery, Moss Brothers. In the cool of the tasting room, the ebullient grape-grower and vintner Jeff Moss held sway, dispensing generous libations of his product. There was no meanness about Jeff's tastings, and it was difficult to drag ourselves away. We were so impressed we bought a mixed case of wine. Although it is easy to be wise after the event, it would seem to me that a policy of more generosity in the tasting department might result in increased sales. I wondered if Jeff could possibly be as cheery as he was all the time if he hadn't been supping on his own sauce—but later found out that he was well-known for his lateral talk and engaging sense of humour. Anyway, if he was enjoying the fruits of his labour as well, why the hell not?

On our way back to our camp at Prevelly Park, Ros cautioned me gently that there were indeed many delightful vineyards in this part of the world but (a) it would not be possible to visit all of them, and (b) we would have to ration the amount of wine we were buying or Penelope's backside would soon be scraping on the ground.

We did make one more detour to the excellent Serventy Organic Vines vineyard, off Rocky Road, which specialises in organically grown wine. There I triumphantly solved the problem of over-loading Penelope by having a case of wine sent directly to Sydney. The Mistress of the Credit Card was won over by tasting a unique rosé-style wine the Serventys call Solstice. We agreed it was the closest thing to bottled sunshine we have ever tasted. To hell with the expense.

As Margaret River was the farthest point west in our journey, we decided to celebrate with dinner at a beach-front restaurant while watching the sun sink into the Indian Ocean. It was time to leave Prevelly Park. Although a delightful camping ground, the summer-holiday crowd had overloaded its less than adequate toilet blocks. By my camping ground measure, it is time to leave when you have to queue for the loo, and spend most of your time in the shower removing plugs of pubic and other hair from the drain so you don't have to stand up to your ankles in someone else's shower juice.

I should say in fairness to Vince the proprietor that he is a splendid and generous fellow. At the beachside restaurant we had met an English lawyer and his wife and sub-teen hyperactive son and less frenetic daughter, who had arrived at Prevelly straight after stepping off an international flight in Perth direct from the UK. It was their first visit to Australia and when they got to Prevelly Park late at night for a week's stay, they found they were double-booked. Not only was the problem solved by Vince taking them into his own family home at no charge, but he also plied them with tucker and the region's finest wines for the entire week. They were, as the English are wont to say, stoked.

There is a touch of sadness in turning our back on the Indian Ocean: although we have the incomparable south-west timber country to explore we are inevitably beginning our homeward journey east. Our plan is to head east over dirt roads to Nannup, then south-east to Manjimup, Pemberton, Walpole, Denmark and on to Albany in King George Sound—where Edward John Eyre ended his epic trek and where Matthew Flinders paused to take on fresh water in *Investigator* before heading east to begin his detailed mapping of much of Australia's southern coast.

The Manor is running sweetly behind Penelope as we slow our speed to cope with rutted and uncertain timber access roads. Not so many years ago this was legendary four-wheel-drive country, much written-up and praised in head-banger periodicals. We plan to lunch at Sue's Bridge (west of Nannup), heavily and lovingly written-up in four-wheel-drive song and story as a great camping spot, well away from conventional vehicles. Well, that was before a new bitumen highway was pushed through from the south, and the ubiquitous CALM fenced off all the good old camping spots and created a picnic ground. As it was a hot day, I took advantage of the delightful free-flowing river to cool off, and as I wiggled my toes among the river stones, imagined the joyous scenes of yesteryear when four-wheel-drivers pitched their tents right beside the river, lit their camp fires, barbecued chops and snags and imbibed plentiful quantities of the brown and bubbly gargle that cheers. I suppose that couldn't go on, with the pressure of progress invading Sue's Bridge, but the bearded winch-and-cable brigade must mourn the good old days and loss of yet another remote spot. Sue's Bridge has become just another politically correct picnic ground, with plastic-lined litter bins bordered with treated pine log barriers.

It has been a terrible summer for bushfires in Western Australia, and we heard on ABC radio that there are fires ahead of us. We are hoping for a bush camp at the end of the day, but that may not be possible. At Nannup we visit the CALM office to find out what is going on, but all the regulars are out fighting fires and the office is presided over by a young man who is just minding the shop and knows nothing. We have heard good reports of a camping spot by a dam at Willow Springs just to the west of the town of Wheatley. There is the smell of smoke in the air, and we are uneasy about stopping at Willow Springs (which turns out to be rather scrubby and unattractive) without knowing more about what the fires are doing.

At the Wheatley general store we found out that we had left the fires behind us, and it was safe to head down the Donnelly Drive towards the One Tree Bridge conservation park and the intriguingly named Greens Island. By 5 pm we were ready to stop, and turned off to Greens Island, which is a former farm, called an island because the floor of the valley is surrounded by creeks—although at this time of the year they contained no water. We had the area to ourselves, though, which is always a bonus.

With a CALM fireplace on hand, we were able to cook our steak, chips and onions on a hotplate and take in the beauty of the forest around us, with no sound other than birdsong. That was until the shooting started, although even the kookaburras seemed to be laughing at the shooters. Still, it was unsettling with vile explosions echoing through the valley. Hoons, or farmers bagging a few foxes and rabbits? They seemed uncomfortably close, although we never saw them. After dinner we sat around our camp fire, entranced by a half moon seeming to weave through scattered high-level clouds. There was hardly a breath of wind, but we could feel the hot forest gradually cooling. I noted in our diary that it was a beautiful and memorable bush camp—perhaps symbolising why we like doing this kind of thing.

Next morning Ros worked out that we have been away five weeks, and only have three weeks left. I don't want to think about it. Turning on to a bitumen road a few kilometres south from Greens Island, we rolled comfortably through delightfully timbered country to Manjimup, a major timber centre dating back to the 1860s. We are heading for Manjimup Timber Park, a ten-hectare celebration of tree murdering. OK, I know timber *is* a renewable resource and we have to have it, but the way it was plundered early this century is scandalous. What the timber-getters would have done if they had had access to chainsaws, bulldozers and electrified timber mills instead of axes, bullock and horse teams and steam-fired boilers to run their pit and bench saws is frightening to think about.

One of the great paradoxes of the timber industry is how much the workers, who cut the trees down, loved the forest. In 1986, the ABC's Bill Bunbury tape-recorded an interview with a former timber man and later conservationist, Jack Tompson, who talked about life as a forester after World War I:

> Our job was timber assessment, and our experience until then had been mostly in jarrah, but when we got down to Pemberton, into the real heart of the king karri country, we saw these magnificent columns rearing into the sky. We'd look at a trunk to assess it for timber value—and volume of timber per acre. We'd look at a log and think, 'Gee, that one is a nice stick'—about ninety-five feet [twenty-nine metres] to where it would be cut off where the crown started to spread. The karri tree is one of the most beautiful trees in the world. Particularly in the primeval forest (what we would call virgin forest) there was a cathedral-like atmosphere. I was writing about it the other day and I described it as being a place where one could hear the myriad musical bird sounds associated with the magnificent atmosphere of a cathedral. This was somewhere where I felt entirely relaxed, and the kind of place I'd always wanted to come back to—that's the way it affected me.
>
> They would send a hundred men out into beautiful virgin jarrah forest and most of them were not very good axemen or good timbermen. I've seen hundreds of trees, twenty years afterwards, that have been felled and left. At one time I got special leave to work with a man who taught me how to cut sleepers and he was one of the greatest timbermen, certainly one of the finest in the country. Anyway he told me he worked for four months once cutting sleepers every day and he never felled one tree; he just followed behind these other fellows who felled beautiful trees and left them. This gives you an idea of the lack of supervision and the waste. Waste in our forests had always been a feature of its exploitation and it still exists today.

Manjimup Timber Park is an excellent place to spend a morning or afternoon, just browsing about. Opened in

1977, it contains a number of historical buildings moved to the site, such as one-teacher schools, and a timber-worker's cottage. (Ros was very taken with a tapestry in the bedroom of the timber-worker's cottage which stitched out a very good philosophy: DON'T WAIT FOR YOUR BOAT TO COME IN—GO OUT AND MEET IT.) The park also has some genuine police cells from the 1940s and there are a fire tower, old timber-getting machinery, great wooden wagons, and steam engines.

In the timber museum there is an arresting 'Time Clock'—a large ring cut from an ancient karri log and set into the museum's western wall. This shows that the tree from which it was cut began life as a seedling in approximately 1600 AD and has been marked with other dates corresponding to important historical events over the last 350 years of human activity. It is a timely reminder of the obscenity of destroying these great living fossils, the karris, which are unique to this small, fertile south-western segment of Western Australia, and only grow where the rainfall exceeds 1016 mm a year.

In his book *Australia's Southwest and our Future*, [Kangaroo Press, Sydney, 1990] the writer and environmentalist Dr Jan Taylor promotes the idea of using genetically engineered bacteria to make cellulose fibres, instead of cutting down trees for woodchips and paper. He believes that future generations of tourists will be aghast at how long we went on cutting these trees down, and simply incredulous that some of the timber should have been used for woodchips. 'The karri forest is a natural heritage which belongs to the world of the future, like the Amazon Basin, and we have no right to go on cutting it for selfish, short-term economic gains.'

The official line on the future of the karri forests from CALM offers somewhat less, as set out in their 1997 publication *A Guide to Karri Country*. 'There are 40 800 hectares of old growth karri set aside in the larger conservation reserves and another 14 600 hectares of old growth karri in road river and stream reserves from which logging is excluded. The management plan adopted by the State Government in 1994, will ensure that the proportion of karri forest in the old growth stage will always be around 40 per cent.'

Feeling like some exercise I climbed the wooden firewatcher's tower, and was admiring the view when the whole structure shuddered. A red-faced man in his sixties was running up wooden ladders to the top like someone possessed. He blurted out a hello, stayed on top for five seconds, and hurled himself down again. I noticed Ros talking to the hyperactive one's wife and it turned out he is such a compulsive personality that when they were planning their holiday she refused to drive across the Nullarbor with him because she knew he would try to pass everything—even road trains. So they flew. She told Ros that it had been like that ever since they were married thirty years ago. At that point he came dashing up to tell his saintly spouse that 'they were behind schedule'. Ros and I felt quite exhausted just witnessing this episode and had to sit down for a while.

The visitors' centre at the Manjimup Timber Park has printed out some 'rules for teachers' of a bygone era which amused us rather.

RULES FOR TEACHERS 1879

1 Teachers each day will fill lamps, clean chimneys before beginning work.

2 Each teacher will bring a bucket of water and a scuttle of coal for the day's session.
3 Make your pens carefully. You may whittle nibs to the individual taste of the children.
4 Men teachers may take one evening a week for courting purposes or two evenings a week to attend church regularly.
5 After ten hours in school, you may spend the remaining time reading the Bible or other good books.
6 Women teachers who marry or engage in unseemly conduct will be dismissed.
7 Every teacher should lay aside from each day, a goodly sum for his benefit during his declining years so that he will not become a burden on society.
8 Any teacher who smokes, uses liquor in any form, frequents pool and public halls, or gets shaved in a barber shop, will give good reason to suspect his worth, integrity, intention and honesty.

RULES FOR WOMEN SCHOOL TEACHERS 1915

1 You will not marry during the term of your contract.
2 You are not to keep company with men.
3 You must be home between the hours of 8 pm and 6 am unless attending school functions.
4 You may not loiter downtown in any of the icecream bars.
5 You may not travel beyond the city limits unless you have the permission of the chairman of the board.
6 You may not ride in a carriage or automobile with any man unless he is your father or brother.
7 You may not smoke cigarettes.
8 You may not dress in bright colours.
9 You must wear at least two petticoats.
10 Your dress must not be any shorter than two inches above the ankle.

11 To keep the school neat and clean you must sweep the floor at least once a day. Scrub the floor at least once a week with hot soapy water. Clean the boards at least once daily and start the fire at 7 am so the school room will be warm by 8 am.

After Manjimup we are planning to camp at Pemberton about fifty kilometres south, another timber town which, apart from its tourist-oriented historical attractions, still has Bunnings Forest Products Mill. This mill actively harvests the local hardwood as it has been doing since 1912 when it won a contract to supply karri sleepers for the transcontinental railway. In an era of dwindling numbers of sawmills, it is still the largest hardwood sawmill in the southern hemisphere.

We did make a slight detour to see the 'Karri with the Hole', as trumpeted in the tourist literature. Some lunatic has taken to a perfectly good karri tree with a chainsaw, and cut a hole through its base big enough to walk through. The tree (rather remarkably I thought) has been able to survive this invasion, but it all seems rather pointless as there are karri trees around (near Pemberton for example) which have natural tunnels through them caused by bygone bushfires.

It is possible to take a short cut down Eastbourne Road which takes you past the famous Diamond Tree Watch Tower about ten kilometres from Manjimup. It was used as a fire lookout from 1941 to 1974 and supports the only wooden treetop tower in the world at a height of 51 metres. It was recently restored and is once again used by CALM as part of its fire management and spotting program. Tourists are also welcome to climb it, up a ladder of steel spikes driven into its flank in a rough imitation of a spiral staircase. As there are no branches to lessen the onset of vertigo until the very top of the tree, I decided to give it a miss, and left it to a young man impressing his girlfriend. My decision was justified when we got to the Pemberton Caravan Park and I saw a man of about my vintage almost fall out of his car, and stagger, half-doubled up, across to the park office with a most singular, crab-like gait. Turns out he was not the victim of childhood paralysis but he had just climbed the Diamond Tree. (Ros also heard a terrifying tale from when the lookout was being refurbished. A young man working on top of the tree dropped a large baulk of timber, which tore out about ten metres of the metal spikes forming the ladder. Unfazed, he simply lowered himself as far as the undamaged spikes on a light rope, and climbed down safely.)

We are to stay for two sleeps in Pemberton to allow Ros an orgy of timber tourism. She claims we have been steaming through the timber country at too smart a pace. Pemberton was farmed from as early as the 1830s, and its timber history dates from 1913 with the cutting of jarrah sleepers for the transcontinental railway. (It is said that many of London's streets were paved with hardwood jarrah blocks from this area.) Pemberton has a plethora of forest walks, adjoining national parks, karri forests, a working tramway and an arboretum. This was first on my horticultural partner's list the following morning. An arboretum is a kind of experimental area where exotic trees are grown to see how they fare in local conditions.

This arboretum was planted half a century ago and included some Canadian redwoods which had done quite well over the years but were clearly not going to make forestry fortunes with softwood. A short walk through the area was a bit disappointing, as it was rather run-down and the trees indifferently identified. One fading sign on a big old karri stump carried some CALM propaganda:

'Decaying stumps like this one remind us that the forest has been carefully regenerated after the original forest was clear fallen for the much needed and valuable timber it contained.' An unimpressed previous walker/conservationist had passed judgment by scrawling over this information with the single word, 'WANK'.

The Gloucester Tree was next on our list—visited by and named after the Duke of, in 1946. It is another of CALM's fire-watching towers and its steel platform is 61 metres from the ground, pipping the Diamond Tree by a good ten metres. Although taller, it does have the psychological advantage of branches sprouting around the steel spike ladder for most of the way.

Ros was heading determinedly off to arts and craft land, to a shop that featured the splendid red jarrah timber crafted into every conceivable object—vases, cutting boards, pastry rollers, serviette rings and so on. There were even jarrah honey-twirlers on offer which I was able to resist.

I found all this unaccustomed heavy touristing quite debilitating—and it was only lunchtime. I managed a quick nap before being urged by Ros into Penelope for the short drive to the beginning of the timber tram ride for two hours of rattling through deep cuttings originally hand-dug by navvies, in two diesel-powered carriages. Our driver and guide was an entertaining young bushie called Sheena, whose droll commentary was delivered so slowly that it was almost as though her personal tape was running slow. Good value though. At a place called

Warren Bridge we were told we had fifteen minutes to walk to see yet another 'karri with a hole'. At least God had created this one with fire, not some chainsawing nutter.

Pausing for an urgent unplanned essential personal purpose, I heard a blast from Sheena's tram whistle, and was so startled I lost my footing and fell over the river bank into some blackberries with my trousers still around my knees. At least I hadn't fallen into the river or, more immediately, something worse. As I half-ran with what remained of my personal dignity back to the Warren Bridge I heard Ros say, 'But my husband is still not back'. Sheena later confessed she nearly lost a whole group one day because they had missed the 'karri with the hole' and just kept going. Again, only their anxious wives prevented a possible stranding.

We had one more destination that long touristy day with which I had no quarrel. Apart from farming and timber, Pemberton is also a wine-growing area, and we had arranged to visit the Gloucester Ridge winery. The owner's wife, Sue, was most gracious and not niggardly with her tastings. Somehow we found ourselves despatching more of the juice of the grape to Sydney. Gloucester Ridge winery is close to the Gloucester Tree, and I noticed that the queue had gone, and some kids who could have been no more than nine or ten were scampering up and down with no evident fear. Why do I feel it necessary to have a go? Dutch courage engendered by Gloucester Ridge unwooded chardonnay? Perhaps there was hope yet for a sexagenarian with incipient vertigo. I decided to come back again in the cool of the following morning to reconsider a climb. Ros thinks I'm silly.

*

I did climb the bloody tree at eight the next morning. Climbers have to negotiate steel spikes hammered into the tree, ascending in a spiral. It was harder and took longer than I thought, and about three-quarters of the way up, with shaking knees and aching wrists, I nearly gave it away. Passing several climbers coming down was tricky. I clung to the spikes closest to the trunk, while they squeezed past. But the view from the top, 61 metres above the ground, was splendid, and I was joined on the fire-watching platform by two young Englishwomen who asked me to take their photos as a memento of the occasion.

I was puzzled why so many of the bigger trees have their tops apparently blasted by lightning, with dead limbs where the apex should be. I found out later that while lightning does occasionally strike these giants, forest fires sometimes get up into the crowns of these fifty-metre plus high karris, and that explains the dead limbs. The trees then sprout new growth around them.

Going down was only marginally less scary. While I was climbing, Ros was talking to Doug, the CALM attendant selling tickets for the climb. The poor chap used to be a farmer but was terribly crippled—I presumed because of a tractor accident or something similar. Having escaped that fate, he seemed determined to smoke himself to death. I asked him if they had 'lost' anybody on the tree.

Lighting up another coffin-nail, Doug said the tally was three, over the years. Two men had heart attacks and died on the tree, and their bodies had to be winched down.

'The third felt crook in the coach, and died in the hotel that night.'

I said I hoped he felt it was worth it.

We are bound for Walpole, which will take us back to the sea and the south coast. On the way we will drive in a tourist loop around the Shannon National Park. That will be our last chance to see substantial stands of karri trees to which we have become mildly addicted. It happens to be the opening day of the marron season—the freshwater lobsters which engender great gastronomic lust in all native denizens of the south-west.

We arrived at the Shannon Dam by late morning and found eager marroners waiting for the clock to tick past noon to throw a variety of meshed and pungently baited traps into the dam. We were tempted to hang around and watch but wanted to make it to Walpole in time to camp. The 'Shannon Loop' is a most engaging drive, through light forest, open country and great stands of towering karri. At the centre of the 'loop' is a camping ground on the site of the now deserted and removed town of Shannon, which supported a timber mill until 1983 and was gazetted as a national park in 1988. One of the more unusual aspects of this drive is that the trees talk to you as you go. This seems reminiscent of 'the Goon Show', and the famous Eccles song sung by Spike Milligan about talking to trees and being locked up for so doing. In this case small, FM transmitters have been hidden away in designated areas, where they deliver information to your car radio. There is a strong oral history component in the tapes and the voices of some of the old foresters who once worked the area add to the effectiveness of the presentation.

One story told by an old-timer that appealed to me was about a new chum who failed to heed good advice from the old hands about what to do if he got lost. The accepted procedure was to give your horse its head, and it would find its way back to camp. This young man who thought he knew better was out in the scrub urging his mount in various directions for three days until hunger and desperation made him give up—and let his horse take him home. He need only have been out a few hours.

On this most delightful drive there are observation points where you can sit quietly and just take in the bird sounds and appreciate the soaring grace of the great karris. We keep seeing signs (a coiled snake) indicating the existence of the Bibbulmun Track. We discovered this is a 180-kilometre bushwalking track from Perth to Walpole on the south coast, traversing many of the region's national parks and taking in large swathes of magnificent timber country. (It turns out the snake symbol is not a friendly warning to bushwalkers, but a representation of Waygal, the rainbow serpent spirit from the Aboriginal Dreaming. The name Bibbulmun is taken from an Aboriginal language group in the south.) It was hoped to have the track extended from Walpole to Albany by the end of 1998.

The walking track was begun in the 1970s by the then Forest Department, and upgraded in the bicentennial year, 1988. In 1993 CALM began a major realignment and upgrade to make it safer and more enjoyable for walkers. Some fifty new camp sites are being built, spaced between ten and twenty kilometres apart—roughly a day's walk—with timber sleeping shelters, tent sites, rainwater tanks, bush toilets, tables and fireplaces. For this trip, though, the Bowdens are doing it the easy way.

We got to Walpole in time to drive to the 'Valley of the Giants' in the late afternoon near Nornalup, where it is possible to walk through the forest canopy of majestic tingle trees on a dramatically engineered series of metal walkways, sitting on top of suspended cables. This treetop walk, only completed very recently, won a prize for design excellence in the 1997 Royal Institute of Architects national awards.

Tingle trees seldom grow more than fifty metres high but have more solid and chunky trunks than the soaring, smooth-barked karris. Twenty years ago, no tour of the south-west was complete without a photograph of your car parked inside the burnt-out interior of a particular giant tingle tree. By 1989, some 100 000 were visiting the valley of the tingle trees each year. In 1990 human impact had not only killed the famous car-accommodating tingle tree, but was threatening the health of the other giants. The rubbing of thousands of human hands had actually polished the bark of some trees, and the vital layers of humus around their roots had disappeared, trampled by visitors' feet.

CALM's Executive Director Syd Shea suggested the area be preserved by constructing a treetop walk (similar to one he had seen in Malaysia) and building elevated timber walkways to protect the immediate environment of the stressed tingle trees. Because the much-visited trees were so degraded, the walkway was built in a new, relatively undisturbed grove of tingle trees close by. The result is a bush and tree experience on a number of levels and is, in my view, the best five bucks' worth you will ever spend.

By far the most dramatic of the walks is through the tree-tops, challenging for anyone with a tendency to vertigo. Children seem immune and race along the swaying metal walkways ignoring the fifty-metre drop to the forest floor beneath their feet and clearly visible through the metal grid of the pathway. Granny, meanwhile, almost paralysed with fear, advances slowly, grimly gripping the handrails and keeping her gaze firmly on the straight and level.

Sadly, one young man was killed during the walkway's construction, falling from one of the slim metal towers that had to be built up from the forest floor to support the cables on top of which the walkway is suspended. This is a breathtaking piece of engineering that means visitors have nothing to distract them from their treetop eyrie; such would not have been the case had the walkway been suspended under the cables in a conventional manner. Ros was enchanted, and we both traversed the walkways twice—at no extra charge. You can walk around ten times if you have the time. Utterly recommended.

We overnighted at Walpole and had less than an hour's run of 55 kilometres along the south coast to Denmark, situated on the Wilson Inlet, a substantial body of sheltered water. With no firm ideas of where we could camp, we drove through the town and turned left along the western bank of the Denmark River to where it meets the estuary. It was still quite early in the morning, a glorious summer day, and there was no wind. There, with the river on one side, and the Wilson Inlet in front, was the most idyllically situated waterfront caravan park we had seen on our entire journey. Before driving in, I noticed two little boys about nine or ten fishing in the Denmark River from a small jetty, watched by their father. A loose circle of pelicans, gulls, and ducks waited expectantly, their reflections perfectly mirrored in the still, dark water. It was a wonderful photograph, and I urged Ros (the official photographer of our expedition) to try to get it.

As she did so I recalled a story I once heard about a similar situation where a man walking along a country river bank came upon two boys, around the same age, fishing. He was struck, as I was in Denmark, at the tranquillity of the moment, and the following dialogue took place.

'Hello boys, catching any fish?' No response.

'They look very fine rods you have there. Were they Christmas presents?' The boys stared straight ahead.

'What bait are you using. Is that a nylon line?'

One of the boys turned to the other.

'Bill—shall I tell him fuck 'im?'

'No, fuck 'im. Tell him nothing.'

Poor Ros, whom I had bullied into trying to take a photograph, came back to Penelope. History almost repeated itself.

'Did you get the photo?'

'I hope so. But as soon as I started taking pictures, one of the boys said: "Daddy, that lady's taking our photograph".'

We scored a waterfront site at the Rivermouth Caravan Park where pelicans and black swans also drifted photogenically by. As I backed The Manor into position with Ros giving directions, I saw her talking to a young girl about eight years old. Then Ros fell about laughing, and left me directionless. When I could, I asked her why she was so amused.

'I said to her, "How long have you been in Denmark?"

'She said, "A week. But we're going back to Australia tomorrow".'

nine

A Whale of a Time

It is only 55 kilometres from Denmark 'back to Australia'—in this case the historic settlement of Albany. We have been looking forward to this phase of the expedition and purposely bypassed King George Sound on our way to Margaret River so we could see Albany properly and spend a few days exploring.

The history here makes Captain Cook's voyage up the east coast seem like yesterday. This part of the coast was first sighted by the Dutch ship *Gulden Zeepaard* (Golden Seahorse) in 1627! It was a VOC ship (Vereenigde Oost-Indische Compagnie) perhaps more conveniently known outside Holland as the United East India Company. The ship was commanded by Frans Thyssen who I feel has rather lost out in the historical stakes to his Very Important Company Passenger, Pieter Nuyts, whose name is featured all along the coast, and whom I have often seen referred to as a 'Dutch navigator'. But he might not have been a navigator at all: I have also seen him called 'a senior company official travelling as a passenger'. If that is really the case, poor old Frans Thyssen probably did the navigating as well as skipper his ship and has fallen a historical victim to his eminent passenger. A more charitable explanation is that only Nuyts would have had the company clout to order Thyssen to take his ship (which was, after all, on a commercial voyage) on such a risky excursion of exploration and discovery so far along the southern coastline of New Holland when he should have been heading for home with his cargo of gold and spices.

In any case we know that the voyage of *Gulden Zeepaard* was the source of the first-known European chart showing the south coast of Western Australia, drawn by the VOC's chief cartographer Hellell Gerritz.

The French may well have visited King George Sound in 1504, but no one is quite sure. The story is a curious one, and outlined in *Albany: Port With a Past and a Future*, by Les Johnson, published by the *Albany Advertiser* in 1997. The good ship *L'Espoir*, captained by one Binot Paulmier de Gonneville, was on a voyage from France to the Indies in 1503, but was caught by a storm somewhere near the Cape of Good Hope and blown way off course. After the tempest, de Gonneville and his shipmates spent several weeks drifting around in fickle winds until they sighted land and found a safe anchorage 'in a pleasant land'. Unfortunately for historians (and French colonial ambitions), de Gonneville's navigation by that stage was so out of kilter that he couldn't say where he'd been. However the hapless navigator did kindle French interest, and for the next 300 years they made various efforts to capitalise on his imprecise discovery.

Kerguelen got close in 1772, after finding and naming the remote sub-Antarctic islands which now bear his name, and reached Cape Leeuwin, but turned north and sailed on to Dirk Hartog Island which he claimed for France. (He died soon afterwards, and that claim died with him.)

The French explorer and navigator La Pérouse may well have seen, or even visited, what would later be called King George Sound when he sailed along the south coast in 1788, but we will never know. After visiting Botany Bay and camping there, he sailed off into oblivion and was never heard of again. Our old friend Admiral Bruny D'Entrecasteaux (who was sent out to look for La Pérouse) at least got a look at the entrance of 'a large bay'—the sound—but was prevented by adverse winds from getting in. He wrote in his log: 'The bay referred to is a beautiful roadstead where vessels of all sizes are able to anchor.'

Meanwhile the British were getting a bit peeved about all this French interest in what they considered their patch and in 1791 sent George Vancouver RN in a sloop of war, *Discovery*, to make sure the Spanish and the French weren't getting too uppity in the Indian Ocean, and to fill in a few navigational gaps as well. Vancouver was no stranger to challenging assignments. He had sailed with the great James Cook on his second and third voyages as a midshipman, and on Friday 13 February 1779—the day before Cook was killed—battled for his own life in the shallows off the same beach against enraged Hawaiians.

Vancouver was forty years old when he was given command of *Discovery* and wrote that ignorance of the southern coast of western New Holland was 'a real blot on geography'. He decided to see what he could do about it. So on 29 September, Michaelmas Day, he was able to report that *Discovery* lay 'snug and secure' in the 'spacious sound' which he had discovered 300 kilometres eastwards of Cape Leeuwin. 'Sound' was a Middle English word meaning, in the nautical sense, a deep inlet from the sea. The 100 square kilometres of Vancouver's discovery—the sound and its two inner harbours—are a magnificent natural safe haven for shipping. It may well be that various whaling captains had used it before Vancouver described it. The whole 'discovery' of King George Sound is veiled in charming uncertainties.

As a result of Vancouver's visit, the British government realised the sound (named after King George III) was the only safe anchorage for shipping in the thousands of kilometres of coast between Shark Bay on the west coast and Melbourne. It was also a port from which the navy could protect one of the richest trade routes in mercantile history from Europe to the Antipodes and Southeast Asia, below 35° latitude.

The French explorer Nicolas Baudin thought so too, after visiting in 1803 and finding an American sealer there. He named the place of their meeting *Port des Deux Peuples* (Port of Two Nations). It is known today as 'Two Peoples Bay', and Ros and I planned to visit it before heading into Albany to find a place to camp.

Baudin wrote enthusiastically about King George Sound and its environs:

> I think it would be difficult to find a place more suitable for the establishment of a colony; in fact I never cease to wonder that the English have not already made one, especially when I reflect that this spot is admirably situated for ships passing directly from Europe to New South Wales, and also for those who wish to go from the Cape to China or the East Indies against the monsoon.

But it was not until almost a quarter of a century later, in 1826, that the British became so jumpy about French interest that they decided to stake a more permanent claim on this superb harbour. On December 25, an expedition of two officers, 18 rank-and-file soldiers, 23 convict workers, one surgeon and a youth, all commanded by Major Edmund Lockyer, arrived on the brig *Amity* from the east coast of Australia (a splendid replica can be seen today on the Albany waterfront) and anchored in the sound. Lockyer did not know whether the French had beaten him to it and was relieved they had the place to themselves. (He had instructions to give the French their marching orders.) The Aborigines were already there, of course, as they had been for thousands of years—but that wasn't considered a problem.

On Boxing Day (Lockyer makes no mention in his diary of its being Christmas Day when they first arrived) they landed and began to settle what became the town of Albany. King George Sound was the only port for the new settlement of Perth on the Swan River (settled three years later in 1929), until the port at Fremantle was developed in 1900.

In 1841 when Edward John Eyre and his sole surviving Aboriginal companion Wylie were heading towards Albany, the settlement had been there for only fifteen years—a modest outpost of British civilisation in a remote corner of the Australian continent. As Ros and I headed east towards the modern Albany, travelling with great comfort in Penelope, I remembered that I had left Eyre and Wylie's narrative when they were in unexpected luxury—after the privations and traumas of their agonising trek around the Great Australian Bight—in the cabin of the obliging Captain Rossiter on the French whaler *Mississippi* near Lucky Bay. But they still had 450 kilometres to negotiate westward before they reached Albany.

When they finally tore themselves away from the hospitable embrace of Captain Rossiter it was June, near midwinter, and bitterly wet and cold. Eyre knew that the worst was behind them, and that they would eventually reach Albany, but they still had to overcome great difficulties. They had gone from never having enough water on the earlier stages of their journey to now having an excess of it—although paradoxically Eyre and Wylie spent a thirsty night two days after they left *Mississippi* because there was no water where they camped, and their water canteens were full of French treacle!

But their morale and optimism were high, in a way which would have been unthinkable only a few weeks before. Eyre wrote in his journal they 'entered upon the continuation of our undertaking with a spirit, an energy and a confidence that we had long been strangers to'.

It was mostly miserable going, having to make painful detours inland to cross swollen streams and creeks, and on 25 June 1841, Eyre wrote a graphic description of their cold, wet ordeal:

> Occasionally the showers came down in perfect torrents, rendering us very cold and miserable, and giving the whole country the appearance of a large puddle. We were literally walking in water; and by stooping down, almost anywhere as we went along, could have dipped a pint pot half full. It was dreadful work to travel thus in the water, and with the wet from the long brush soaking our clothes for so many hours . . .

Five days later, Eyre told Wylie that he would soon see the hills around King George Sound and, when they came in sight, 'his joy knew no bounds. For the first time on our journey he *believed* we should really reach the Sound at last.' But it took another cold and clammy week before Eyre and Wylie looked down—in the rain—at what seemed to be the deserted settlement of Albany. Just before, Wylie had met one of his countrymen who greeted him with great joy. He told the explorers that they had been expected two months before, and since then Wylie had been 'mourned for and given up as dead by his friends and tribe'.

As they gazed down on the town, Wylie's Aboriginal friend shouted 'a wild joyous cry', which he repeated again and again, announcing Wylie's return from the dead. Eyre described how the streets, which had appeared before 'so gloomy and untenanted, were now alive with natives—men, women and children, old and young, rushing rapidly up the hill, to welcome the wanderer on his return, and to receive their lost one almost from the grave'.

Eyre was most moved by the scene, and his own instinctive humanity towards Aboriginal people—not shared, sadly, by many of his fellow Europeans in those days—is evident from his journal:

> Affection's strongest ties could not have produced a more affecting and melting scene—the wordless weeping pleasure, too deep for utterance, with which he was embraced by his relatives, the cordial and hearty reception given him by his friends, and the joyous greeting bestowed upon him by all, might well have put to the blush those heartless calumniators, who, granting the savage as the creature only of unbridled passions, deny to him any of those better feelings and affections which are implanted in the breast of all mankind, and which nature has not denied to any colour or to any race.

Eyre went straight to the house of a Mr Sherratt, whose family he had stayed with when he was in Albany the year before, and after a glass of 'hot brandy and water', a bath and a change of clothes, was able to feel 'comparatively comfortable'—which seems an uncharacteristic understatement for that particular moment.

There was also some essential business to attend to. Eyre made a sworn deposition on Baxter's death and wrote a summary of his journey for a delighted Western Australian government which promised, on Eyre's urging, to reward Wylie's loyalty with a lifetime's supply of rations. Six days after he had ridden into town, Eyre was on his way by ship to Adelaide. This journey took only thirteen days. It was more than a year since he had set out from Adelaide, first to try to penetrate north into the interior, and then west on his coastal odyssey.

Eyre and Wylie would never meet again, but Eyre did not forget his loyal companion. Seven years later, when Eyre was Lieutenant Governor of New Zealand, he heard that the Western Australian government had not honoured its promise to keep Wylie supplied with weekly rations, and wrote a long letter to the governor which ensured Wylie did receive them, as far as is known, to the end of his days.

Although Eyre had brought the South Australian colonists no news of rich pastures or minerals which might help to save the bankrupt colony, he was warmly welcomed to Adelaide and feted as a hero. His westward journey might have been judged an economic failure, but by any standards it was a great geographical triumph. Eyre had discovered and examined unknown country 400 kilometres to the north and 1600 kilometres to the west—and he was the first explorer to see the country beyond the cliffs recorded by Matthew Flinders. Although Governor Grey had just replaced Eyre's mentor, Governor Gawler, and Grey's own confident prediction of stock routes to the west was clearly now a nonsense, he was generous to Eyre and praised his 'dauntless courage'.

The Royal Geographical Society in London thought he deserved recognition too, awarding him its Founder's Medal—the first given for Australian exploration—in May 1843.

Two Peoples Bay, where the Frenchman Baudin met the American sealing captain in 1803, is about 35 kilometres to the east of Albany, and tucked in behind the appropriately named Cape Vancouver. We guided Penelope and The Manor around the top of Oyster Harbour until we entered the Two Peoples Bay Nature Reserve. Had it not been for the noisy scrub bird, this beautiful area would have been turned into a satellite township in the early 1960s. But after it was surveyed in 1961, a distinctive bird call was heard in thick vegetation. It was the long-lost noisy scrub bird, thought to have been extinct since 1889. During the early days of settlement the noisy scrub bird had been widespread in dense scrub and swamps on the edge of forest areas around Albany, but was thought not to have survived the new settlers' burning, grazing, and drainage of swamps.

However, an isolated population of the rare birds survived at Two Peoples Bay probably because nearby Mt Gardner acted as a shield against bushfires in summer. After the area had been reclassified as a reserve, the noisy scrub bird population increased, from about 40 singing males in 1962 to 200 in 1987. So successful has the preservation program been that birds have been taken to other reserves with the right habitat. Apart from the recovery of the noisy scrub bird from apparent extinction, a delightful wilderness area has been preserved for future generations. Two Peoples Bay is a beautiful beach sheltered from the prevailing south-westerly, bordered with the smooth worn-down granite rocks so typical of the area. We walked over South Point to Little Beach, which is more private, and not immediately obvious to visitors. We had it to ourselves, and sat for a time on the sand, watching the white caps of the waves whipped away from the shore across the sound by the stiff south-westerly. Near the beach, the water was the clearest turquoise blue that can be imagined. Later, we would be reminded of this beautiful spot in a most unexpected and pleasant way.

On our way out from Albany we had noticed signs for a marron farm, so we called in. The freshwater crustaceans are matured in a series of circular tanks that look like above-ground swimming pools. Perhaps they are. The cheerful proprietor seemed happy enough to take us around, and then scoop out six marrons for our evening meal. (We had to have a certificate from him confirming that the local delicacy had not been nicked from someone's dam out of season.) He also told us that marrons have the unique ability to live for eight hours out of water by using their gills to breathe through water stored in their heads. The most humane way to kill them, he said, was to drown them in salty water before cooking.

We camped at a caravan park at Emu Point, just near the beach and not too far from the centre of Albany which we had yet to visit. There was a message waiting for us at the office from our friends from Thomas River, the Williamses. The message not only described where they were camping, but attached the battered label from the $2 muscat as a memento—the very same vino that doubled as brake fluid and later desperation gargle for a grogless Greg.

'Cocktails at six and stay for dinner' was the rest of the message. How could we resist. A quick trip to the fishing co-op for some local mussels as our contribution to the meal seemed a good idea. We steamed them open and pulled off those little hairy, twatty bits that mussels have. We expected to be almost carried away by bushflies during this operation—but not so. Someone on the road told us there were no flies in Albany, and it must be true. Why the ubiquitous, sticky, nostril-invading Western Australian bushfly has given this area a miss is a puzzle. We weren't complaining, I might say.

Then a joyous reunion with Heather, Greg, Todd and Ryan at the Middleton Beach Caravan Park where they have scored a beachfront site for their caravan—without power—in return for Greg doing some refrigeration repairs and other handyman jobs. Some cheerful 'grey nomads', and fellow caravan-park workers were also sitting out under the caravan awning attacking Heather's hommos dips and enjoying a convivial glass. Six-year-old Ryan had been augmenting his pocket money by scouring the beach for shells to sell to tourists. He offered me one of his best specimens, which was generous. I wanted to give him ten cents but Heather wouldn't let me!

There had been a bit of drama in the caravan park earlier in the day. An arriving grey nomad, tired and harassed at the end of a long day's haul, was in the act of backing his large van on to a parking slab when the poor chap had a heart attack. His wife helped him into the caravan where he collapsed on a bed—and that made it difficult for the ambulance crew to carry him out through the door on a stretcher. As the emergency lads were discussing their problem, the patient piped up and said: 'Well, I've managed to get corpses out of much more difficult spots than this.' It turned out the coronary case was an undertaker by trade, and not averse to some black humour. His wife, it was quickly realised, was not very competent in the camping department (her husband normally did all the practical things) but the local community rallied around and made sure her van and awning were properly established, and involved her in local activities to keep her spirits up. The latest news from the hospital was that her undertaker partner was not planning to give any extra work to the local parlours, and was expected to make a good recovery.

(It reminded me of a similar accident that happened with a party of venerable Australian ex-prisoners of war who were on a pilgrimage to Thailand in 1984, to visit part of the Thai-Burma Railway they had been forced to build for the Japanese during World War II. I was travelling with them for the ABC, and as we arrived at Bangkok airport, one ex-POW collapsed between Immigration and Customs and died from a heart attack. I was surprised—but shouldn't have been I suppose—at the calm and matter-of-fact way his companions reacted to this tragedy. They were no strangers to sudden death, and had seen many of their comrades die of starvation, cholera, malaria or beri-beri during the war. They efficiently contacted the

Australian Embassy to arrange for the body to be sent back to Australia, and continued on their excursions making sure that the dead man's wife was included and kept busy and occupied. 'Jack always wanted to come back to Thailand,' said one of his mates cheerfully. I felt Jack might have wanted to have seen a bit more of it than just the airport before handing in his cheque. At least he had managed to clear Immigration before collapsing. Had he died before officially entering the country, an Embassy bloke confirmed, the administrative complications would have been horrendous.)

Over dinner we caught up with the Williamses. As it was necessary to replenish their coffers, they planned to stay in Albany for at least three months while Greg juggled two jobs. We arranged to meet the next afternoon to see Whaleworld, one of Albany's biggest tourist attractions, which was a working whale-catching and processing operation until as late as 1978, and is now a popular museum. It had the dubious distinction of being the last shore-based whaling enterprise in the southern hemisphere.

After claiming our mail, we had a drive around the centre of Western Australia's oldest settlement. The rounded tower of the convict-built post office looked vaguely like part of a fantasy castle in a Disneyland—or so it seemed to me. The Albany Residency Museum is near the waterfront, not far from the replica of the brig *Amity*, and was built in the 1850s as a convict store. It is now part of a museum complex that also offers a spectacular display featuring the original crystal and prism light from the Eclipse Island lighthouse. No charge for admission either.

The town hall, first opened in 1888, is another fine colonial building. We drove up to the top of Mt Clarence, which not only gives splendid views of Albany and King George Sound but is the site of a vigorous bronze sculpture, life-size, of horses urged on by their soldier riders, rearing and plunging in the heat of battle. It is a memorial to Australians who served in the Desert Mounted Corps in World War I, was originally erected in Suez in 1932, but was badly damaged by the ungrateful Egyptians when Britain invaded the canal zone during the short-lived 1956 Suez War. The horses and their riders have actually been recast from the original damaged metal, but the granite rocks on which they stand are originals, and the bullet marks scarring them are too. The memorial seems oddly incongruous in that isolated, elevated bushland setting.

Albany is still awash with whale oil. Although Ros and I have now given up on beach fishing this trip, even our caravan park kiosk is offering plastic bottles of whale oil to mix with bran as bait or berley. I was told there are 44-gallon drums of the stuff stashed away in back sheds all over town.

When you first catch a glimpse of the former whaling station at Frenchman Bay, 20 kilometres east of Albany, it is easy to understand why. It is staggering to think that the five enormous storage tanks were once all full to the brim with whale oil. They are so massive they look as though they should be part of a petrol refinery. Some idea of their size can be gauged by the way they are being developed today as part of the whaling museum. Several are being fitted with internal spiral staircases, with artefacts and photographs to view as you climb up, and a lookout at the top through observation windows cut through the heavy steel plating.

Freelance whaling began in Albany possibly before King George Sound was officially discovered by Captain

George Vancouver in 1791, and American whaling fleets operating from New Bedford and Bridgeport, in Massachusetts, used the sheltered waters of the sound for their operations through most of the nineteenth century. Cheynes Beach, sheltered from the prevailing southwesterlies, was a popular spot to boil down the blubber hacked from sperm whales for oil. The site was named after an Albany pioneer, George Cheyne, who was involved with that early industry. In 1952 the Cheynes Beach Whaling Company began operations, and continued for the next 26 years—until 1978.

We have been invited to Whaleworld by its present manager, Les Bail, a cheerful, bearded ex-professional scuba diver and charter-boat operator who was born and bred in Albany and has a fierce love and appreciation of its history and wild coastlines. Les Bail was one of a number of charter-boat operators who took tourists out to see the southern right, sperm and humpback whales which kept swimming along the coast past King George Sound on their way to the Great Australian Bight and other warm-water breeding grounds as their instincts had always compelled them to do, and as their numbers built-up. In 1989 he was issued with the first commercial whale watch licence in Western Australia—although he had been operating charter boats among whales since 1982.

When whaling stopped, John Bell (who had flown spotter aircraft to guide the company's three whale chasers to their prey) and his wife, Jill, opened a small museum and a souvenir shop to encourage tourists to visit the site of Australia's last operating whaling operation—leased by the Jaycees Community Foundation who planned to develop

Whaleworld as a tourist attraction with help from both federal and state governments. An important and spectacular addition to the site was the beaching in 1982 (using Bell's engineering skills) and positioning of *Cheynes IV*, one of the company's chasers, whose flared black bows now tower over visitors to the museum.

John Bell and Les Bail met under unusual circumstances on 16 May 1988. Les and two companions were returning from a diving trip to Doubtful Islands, 99 nautical miles east of Albany, in his boat *Ondine* when she unexpectedly sank. They managed to get a 'mayday' call out, and John Bell flew down in his Cessna 172 and located them. He circled above the three men, waggling the wings of his aircraft to alert the rescue vessel to their position. Les thought it only right to take a couple of bottles of wine around to Bell's house to say thanks. Bell insisted the two men demolish them there and then. The pilot told Les Bail that he was the only person he had helped to rescue (and there were many) who had ever bothered to come and say thanks! A firm friendship was forged.

One of Bell's most spectacular rescues took place in 1965 off the coast after alerting a whale chaser to available whales. He was running low on fuel and had actually turned for home in his float plane when he received a call on his radio from the ship:

'The skipper's lost his leg. Any chance of a lift?'

The whale-chaser captain, Ches Stubbs, had unwittingly put his foot into a loop of rope just as he fired the harpoon gun into a whale. His foot was taken off cleanly, just above the ankle. Bell, interviewed for the Battye Library in 1989, recalled what happened then:

> There was a pretty big swell running . . . and I made a quick decision that I would land and then have another look at the situation once I was on the water . . . because it always looks a lot calmer from up there than when you're sitting on it. So I did that. I landed, and still decided it was going to be touch and go.

By then committed to the rescue, Bell threw out his emergency rubber dinghy, which was used to transport the injured skipper, paddled by another crewman. To Bell's surprise, once the skipper was on board, the crewman climbed in too. So instead of an aircraft designed for one person, he had three on board. Bell did try a take-off run, but abandoned it quickly as hopeless. He taxied back towards the ship and dropped the crewman off near the rubber dinghy (only finding out much later that the poor chap could not swim).

> While this was going on I remembered reading somewhere—being a bit of a fanatic on seaplane operation—[about] a technique used during the war in the open sea in conjunction with ships. If you got them to do a high speed run and then a quick turn at the end of it, it had the effect of flattening out the sea for a certain area.

Bell asked the ship to attempt this manoeuvre and, following in the whale-chaser's track, managed to take-off after one further failed attempt.

> It was only then, looking down, I saw a bit of colour in the water; and I thought that's strange, that's the same colour as some of the parts of this aeroplane. [Laughs]. I still wasn't sure what I was looking at, and when we got home I found out that we'd left a wingtip behind! As we'd fallen off one of the swells on the first attempt to take off, the aircraft slewed around into the wind, and at the same time sort of

> heeled over, and the wingtip smacked the water and just wiped the fibreglass tip away . . . it had no effect on the flying. And when we got back and had a look at the aircraft, we found that the whole wing had wrinkled—severely wrinkled—to the point where it had to be renewed. All very interesting . . .

The skipper made a good one-legged recovery, and Bell received a well-deserved award for bravery.

Ever versatile, Bell stopped being the poacher and turned gamekeeper after whaling ended in 1978. He used his Cessna to make aerial assessments of increasing numbers of the formerly hunted humpback and southern right whales along the coast, taking off from a short airstrip just behind Whaleworld.

In March 1996, the lives of Les Bail and John Bell intersected again in tragic circumstances. Bell and three passengers died in a plane crash at sea, while the pilot was allegedly helping federal authorities combat drug smuggling. Les Bail was asked to take over as manager of Whaleworld until the Jaycees Community Foundation could be properly organised. He is still there.

Ever since he dived with and photographed whales, and then took tourists out by charter boat to see them, Les has been fascinated by these gentle giants. Looking back, he sees managing Whaleworld as a natural continuation of his interests. In 1982, working with Bell, he had helped to scuttle one of the whale chasers, *Cheynes III*, off Michaelmas Island in King George Sound where it has become a Mecca for divers from all over the world. Before it was sunk, a group of volunteers recovered its triple expansion steam engine which was reassembled and set up at Whaleworld with an electric motor demonstrating how it worked.

The beached chaser *Cheynes IV* was closed to the public in 1994 for safety reasons, but Les is working on a project to re-open it for tours in 1999. Other major work has been the restoration of the timber flensing deck, where the whales were cut up before being processed. In 1998 the former factory was declared a Western Australian Heritage icon, and has been entered in the Register of Historic Places.

Although Whaleworld is now a fascinating museum dedicated to the celebration and preservation of whales, it is set against a chilling background of death, with all the evidence of that cruel trade displayed, from flensing decks and massive processing machinery to vicious looking harpoon guns with explosive heads, and maps showing the position and type of all whales killed over the years. A veritable forest of pins and dots.

As a bonus, there is a remarkable display of historic aircraft at the rear of the former whaling processing plant. This was organised by John Bell who managed to obtain a selection of vintage aircraft for his Malcolm Green Aviation Museum, first opened in 1992. A magnificent Catalina flying boat takes pride of place and I was also intrigued to see a Vought-Sikorsky VS-310 Kingfisher float plane. I was even more interested when I learned of its origins from Les. This was the same aircraft that was taken to Antarctica in the first postwar attempt by Australia to establish a base on the continent. I had seen photographs of it mounted, incongruously, on the deck of a tiny 500 tonne wooden former Norwegian herring trawler named *Wyatt Earp*. HMAS *Wyatt Earp* no less! This ship had been used by the American millionaire Lincoln Ellsworth in his many attempts to be the first expedition to fly across the

Antarctic continent—an ambition finally realised in 1939. He had named the expedition ship after his boyhood hero, the legendary marshal of Dodge City. In 1948 it was the only vessel available with any capacity to operate in pack ice, and it was refurbished by the Australian Navy and sent south with the Kingfisher mounted amidships.

The voyage was unsuccessful. It was the last time a national Antarctic expedition set forth in a wooden ship with sails. *Wyatt Earp* leaked, broke down and had two false starts before having to give up in March 1948 and return to Melbourne. The Kingfisher only flew on one day of the trip, in sheltered water behind a big iceberg north of the Balleny Islands. The business of fitting its folded wings, and getting it on and off the ship was simply too cumbersome and difficult. I became aware of this aircraft while researching my book *The Silence Calling—Australians in Antarctica 1947–97*, a history written for the jubilee of ANARE (Australian National Antarctic Research Expeditions). So it was a great delight accidentally to come upon the actual aircraft in John Bell's collection.

There were other Antarctic memories stirred that day. Les's wife Dorothy is the sister of Alison Clifton, whose place in ANARE history is as the first woman Station Leader to take up her duties—on Macquarie Island in 1989. In fact it was Alison who had suggested to me that we look up Les and Dorothy in Albany and they, following our Whaleworld excursion, invited the Williamses and the Bowdens to dinner. A hilarious evening resulted, during which it must be admitted copious quantities of excellent local Mt Barker grape juice were ingested, Les showed us some of his remarkable slides of close encounters with whales, underwater and from the surface.

We also talked about Albany's weather. Earlier in the day a stiff south-westerly had been whipping spray across the bay from the shelter of the hills behind Frenchman Bay. It is high summer, and not surprisingly the best weather of the year, although windy. One of the Whaleworld's guides had a good line on Albany climate. He pointed across to Breaksea Island, shining in the sun.

'When you look out into King George Sound and see Breaksea Island all sunny and crystal clear—you know it's going to rain. When you can't see the islands—it is raining.'

We can linger no longer, as we have to be back in Sydney by the end of January. We have had our final 'cocktails' until God-knows-when with the Williamses. Heather gave Ros some recipes for her magic sauces and crepes, and Greg produced a magnificent landscape photograph of Two Peoples Bay which he had specially enlarged for us—the very scene we had marvelled at only days before. It will be an enduring memory of a special time, and a celebration of a friendship we all know will continue, that began during our chance meeting at Thomas River. The two boys, Todd and Ryan, seemed genuinely sorry to see two old buzzards like us leave their lives. We certainly were. One day they will have to face the twenty-first century, when they stop being gypsies. We hoped the impact of the real world wasn't going to be too painful.

For the first time we are retracing our steps. First east, along the coast to Esperance, and then north to Norseman—which we have not yet visited, having cut down to the south coast from Balladonia on our way across the Nullarbor. Wheat harvesting is going on, although we hear on the radio that there are hot gusty winds and fires. We had toyed with the idea of heading north before Esperance, up to Lake King and then east along a dirt road to meet up with the main highway again south of Norseman, but with fires mentioned in the area we gave it a miss.

There are some wonderful place names in Australia. After turning north from Esperance we ran through Gibson's Soak, and the Gibson's Soak Hotel. Perhaps named after a legendary tosspot? My middle name is Gibson. We may have been related.

By late afternoon we could see a huge thunderhead building up to the west. As we got closer to Norseman we could see it was a great pillar of smoke. The policeman's wife (working in the newsagency) was kind enough to make a radio call to call her husband, who was away helping to fight the fires. She confirmed that the road from Lake King had been closed. Had we come that way, we would have been stranded. There were some thundery clouds about too, and a few spatters of rain, but not enough to help the firefighters.

Norseman is a service town for those crossing the Nullarbor. I asked at our caravan park about the quality of the local water and was intrigued to hear it came from Perth, via Boulder and Kalgoorlie. The pipeline is 800 kilometres long and, perhaps not surprisingly, Norseman is as far east as the Perth water goes. We topped up The Manor's water tank and refuelled Penelope ready for the morning. We had planned to eat out, but the receptionist at the rather chintzed-up motel we went to was snooty about our taking in our own bottle of red wine, so we retreated to The Manor and cooked what was almost certainly a better pasta with tomato and garlic sauce than we would have scored at the pretentious motel. Strolling around after dark, I was struck by the number of car transports getting ready to leave for the west and, indeed, arriving from the east. Did we not have a transcontinental railway? I asked one of the drivers why so many cars were going by road and he all but exploded at my ignorance.

'We take them by road both ways so we can get them there undamaged. If they go on the train they get bumped in transit, and covered with abrasive brake dust from the train, and that's not the half of it. Recently one rail truck went off the rails and wrote off ninety new vehicles. And, apart from that, it's more economical to send them by road. *That's* why we do it. It takes five days each way.'

I thanked him and withdrew. Those truckies on the long hauls sure earn their money. I hope it's enough.

The weather is cooling down. With luck we may have our second cool crossing of the Nullarbor in high summer.

ten

The Last Bush Camp

If all goes to plan, we will have our longest day's run of the whole trip today. We got away from Norseman at 6 am and hit our cruising speed of 110 kph with The Manor running smoothly behind. The weather is looking stormy, but it is unseasonably cool for our crossing. ('Crossing the Nullarbor' seems to be a generic term for the run from Norseman to Ceduna—some 1200 kilometres—rather than the relatively short span across the designated 'Nullarbor National Park' near the South Australian border, which is less than 200 kilometres.)

We have travel rules that preclude driving at night. That is when you bang into kangaroos and other nocturnal bush animals or livestock. According to the famous signs seen near Ceduna, it is possible to score a triple—a camel, an emu and a roo. So our run today of over 800 kilometres before sunset is ambitious. We will not stop, except to pee and change drivers every two hours, and munch our lunch of prepacked sandwiches on the run. We are planning to camp out tonight—our last bush camp of the trip. Although our noses are definitely pointing towards the stable door there is a certain sadness in the realisation that the end is in sight. Half an hour out, we have a strong headwind that is pegging us back to 105 kilometres per hour. Ros is worried about an odd noise that seems to be coming from the engine.

'It's as though something is flapping loose.'

'Toyota Landcruiser engines don't have things that flap loose.'

But I could not source it either.

Half an hour later we both realised what it was. We had started off with the radio on the local ABC, and had run out of range. The radio was crackling and spluttering, and could just be heard over the engine and wind noise. End of problem.

The grass on the verges of both sides of the highway has been burnt off. It reveals a ghastly trail of bottles and junk hurled out of passing cars or trucks.

I was told that truckies buy large bottles of soft drink. After drinking them, they pee in them, and chuck them out the window so they don't have to lose time stopping for a toilet break. Perhaps it is a road myth. I hope so.

We have a camp site in mind, if we can make it, which we noted on the way over. It had a water tank for travellers, and plenty of scope to drive off amongst mallee scrub to be out of sight of the road. It is just before the Eyre Highway reaches the lookout points on the great waterless cliffs of the Great Australian Bight that caused our old friend Edward John such problems on his way across the Nullarbor in 1841.

I have been doing some reading about what happened to Eyre after the triumph of his crossing from South Australia to King George Sound. After he returned to

Adelaide, Governor Sir George Grey appointed him resident magistrate and protector of Aborigines at Moorundie, in South Australia, where he served for four years. As one would expect from his enlightened dealing with the first Australians on his overland trek, he was a compassionate and progressive administrator. He was still anxious to do more exploring, particularly north into the interior, which had defeated him before he turned west to Albany. He volunteered several times to lead a new expedition, but it was considered Thomas Mitchell had greater claims.

In 1845 he returned to England, where he published his *Journals of Expeditions of Discovery into Central Australia and Overland from Adelaide to King George's Sound in the Years 1840–1*, and met the young woman whom he would later marry, Fanny Osmond. From England any hopes of further Australian journeys were dashed when he heard that the exploration efforts of Charles Sturt and Ludwig Leichhardt had solved the geographical mystery of Australia's 'dead heart'. Eyre never returned to Australia to live, but whether this was simply because he was not offered any post or position there, or out of disappointment at the lack of further exploration opportunities, can only be guessed at.

He was, however, offered the post of Lieutenant-Governor of New Zealand in 1846, which he did accept. He conducted some long-distance correspondence with Fanny Osmond in England which was successful, and his bride voyaged to Wellington to marry him. It was during his six-year term in New Zealand that he discovered his former Aboriginal companion Wylie had not been accorded the rations promised him, and did something about it.

Eyre was so highly thought of after his service in New Zealand that he was appointed Lieutenant-Governor of the island of St Vincent in the West Indies in 1854, Acting-Governor of the Leeward Islands in 1860, and then Acting Governor of Jamaica. In Jamaica he was involved in putting down a Negro mutiny and hanging a member of the local legislature, G W Gordon. Gordon was a revolutionary who conspired to overthrow the British administration and form a new West Indian Republic, with the help of a Haitian General and arms and ammunition to be obtained from the USA. He had instigated a massacre at a place named Stony Gut, near Morant Bay on 11 October 1865 during which all the inhabitants—including 22 officers and men of the volunteer force—were slaughtered. The official reaction was severe, and in the reprisals that followed, the total number of executions passed 400.

Eyre, in the hot seat, was recalled to England and three times tried for his actions, but was acquitted each time. Virtually admitting that Eyre had been harshly done by, the British Parliament approved the payment of his legal expenses from the public purse in 1872, and two years later he was granted the pension usually accorded a colonial governor in retirement.

It was ironic, in view of Eyre's enlightened views on Aborigines and blacks, that he should have been so pilloried for what was a political, not a racial matter. In any event the Anti-Slavery Committee took up his cause and formed the 'Eyre Defence Fund'. Eyre maintained a dignified front through the years of litigation, but it must have been an enormous disappointment after his otherwise distinguished career. He just made it into the new century and died in Devonshire, England, on 30 November 1901, survived by his wife Fanny, four sons and a daughter.

'While we're tying up loose ends', said Ros, 'what happened to Matthew Flinders after he finished his Australian explorations?'

'That story can best be told through his cat.'

Like his distinguished predecessor, Captain James Cook, Matthew Flinders' writing and journals were fairly formal affairs, giving only glimpses of what manner of man he was. By the standards of the day he seems to have been an exceptionally considerate captain, and maintained the friendships made on his many voyages during his all-too-short life. Fascinating glimpses of Flinders' personality, and of life on one of His Majesty's ships at the beginning of the nineteenth century are given in an affectionate little memoir he wrote about the ship's cat, Trim.

Trim made two voyages to Australia, only to fall foul of the French with his master when Flinders was incarcerated in 1803 at Mauritius, where he had called in on his way back to England to have his leaking schooner *Cumberland* repaired. (He did not know that war had broken out between England and France.) Flinders survived his seven-year confinement, but Trim did not adapt to a landlubber's life, disappearing in 1804 without trace on the island, in his prime and aged a modest four years. The memory of this feisty feline has been commemorated by a bronze statue, which stands on a windowsill of the Mitchell Library in Sydney just behind a statue of Flinders which was unveiled (appropriately) by Rear Admiral David Campbell of the Royal Australian Navy at a well-attended ceremony in 1996. A small book reprinting Flinders' catty tribute was published by Angus & Robertson the following year.

According to Flinders, Trim was an exceedingly handsome creature whose 'robe was a clear jet black, with the exception of his four feet which seemed to have been dipped in snow, and his underlip which rivalled them in whiteness. He had also a white star on his breast and it seemed as if nature had designed him for the prince and model of his race'.

As a shipboard kitten, Trim's antics often caused him to fall overboard, but he was not bothered by water, and learned to swim and run up any rope that was thrown down to rescue him. He was allowed to sit at table with both officers and men (Trim dined first in the officers' mess) and was offered titbits from time to time. If an officer was silly enough to hold a morsel on his fork and wave it about while talking, Trim 'would ship it off the fork with his paw, on its passage to the mouth, with such dexterity and an air so graceful that it rather excited admiration than anger'.

Flinders noted that while in New South Wales waters, 'Bongaree, an intelligent native of Port Jackson, was also on board our little sloop; and with him Trim formed an intimate acquaintance'. Trim, though, was rather imperious with his Aboriginal friend. 'If he had occasion to drink, he mewed to Bongaree and leaped up to the water cask; if to eat he called him down below and went straight to his kid [a sailor's wooden tub for grog or rations], where there was generally a remnant of black swan.'

As noted, Trim came to grief on Mauritius, and was never found despite an offered reward of ten Spanish dollars. Flinders had his own ideas about what happened: 'It is but too probable that this excellent unsuspecting animal was stewed and eaten by some hungry black slave, in whose eyes all his merits could not be balanced against the avidity excited by his sleek body and fine furred skin.'

'Thus', concluded Flinders, 'perished my faithful intelligent Trim! The sporting, affectionate and useful companion of my voyages during four years. Never, my Trim, "to take thee all in all, shall I see thy like again"; but never wilt thou cease to be regretted by all who had the pleasure of knowing thee.'

The grieving navigator vowed to build a memorial to his cat if he ever settled down in 'a thatched cottage, surrounded by half an acre of land'. But Flinders' health was so debilitated by his seven years on Mauritius that he only lived another four years with his beloved wife who had waited so long in England for him, a personal drama captured movingly by Ernestine Hill in her novel, *My Love Must Wait*.

So the only memorial to Trim sits, not near a thatched cottage, but on the windowsill of Sydney's Mitchell Library—in the continent that both Trim and Flinders were the first to circumnavigate.

The sun was getting low as we cruised past Eucla and on to the South Australian border. Coming from this direction we don't have to surrender our fruit and vegies until we reach Ceduna some time tomorrow. There was, however, an unfortunate incident. Ros was driving and because there was traffic coming the other way she had no alternative but to run over the carcass of a very mature kangaroo.

From experience we now know that it is best not to

run over dead and rotting kangaroos dead-centre. It is best to try and keep the carcass a little to one side of Penelope's track. This is because the tow bar and safety chains underneath the back bumper are the lowest point. There was a distinct bump and shudder as we connected with the deceased roo. I feared we had begun an unwanted and continuing association, and I was dead right—as it were.

Stopping for fuel at the Border servo, I got out of the car into a black swarm of delighted blowflies. The tow bar and chains had gouged great gobbets of rotten flesh from the departed kanga. These had not only splattered all over the chains and tow bar, but back against the front of The Manor. The look was bad and the smell was vile. Not only that, but the rushing dry wind had begun to turn the meat into repulsive roo jerky, defying any immediate effort to hose the stuff away. There was no obvious solution to this putrid mess, so we simply closed up the windows, fired up the airconditioning and drove on.

'As we are now in South Australia', said my life's partner, 'what do your exploration books say about my great-great-grandfather Charles Bonney after he and Joseph Hawdon drove cattle overland to Adelaide from New South Wales in 1838?'

'I can only tell you that he moved about a bit, first to Melbourne and then back to South Australia, became a magistrate and Commissioner for Crown Lands and married your great-great-grandmother, one Charlotte Heritage.

'He went into politics in 1857, as the member for East Torrens, and became Commissioner for Lands, resigned in 1858 and went to England. He was back in 1869 as general manager of the South Australian railways, but by 1871 he was appointed Inspector of Lands. When he retired in 1880 he moved to Melbourne, and then finally to Sydney where he died in 1897 at the respectable age of 84—survived by your great-great-grandmother Charlotte and five of his nine children.'

'It seems a long time since we first thought about him at Lake Bonney', said Ros. 'But it was only six weeks ago.'

The sun was low by the time we spotted the sign leading to the water tank and bush camping area. Although we have been working by the sun today, we have actually lost two-and-a-half hours between Western and South Australia. Our speedo showed 866 kilometres—certainly our longest day's run to date. We were keen to get well away from the highway, not just for security's sake, but because of the noise of road trains thundering through the night. A maze of tracks led through the mallee scrub where other travellers had gone before.

We jumped out to crank up The Manor—and almost jumped back into Penelope again. The kangaroo meat had dried out to the point where the bushflies were less interested, but the area was swarming with March flies, which were intensely interested in us! Putting up The Manor was punctuated with slaps and swearing. These flies specialise in targeting the backs of legs so when you have both hands full doing something they bite you when you can't kill them. They are also slow to react and relatively easy to swat. But they do have a painful sting.

'These are historical flies', I muttered to Ros through clenched teeth. 'Our old pal Edward John Eyre mentioned them as "horse flies". They drove the horses mad as well as the explorers.'

Mercifully they were not interested in following us inside, and the cold ales from The Manor's fridge had never tasted so good from within the fly-screened interior. And the flies had the decency to disappear when the sun set.

We toasted our last bush camp—and all the explorers who had gone before us. The sunset was a beauty (which we felt was only our due on this rather special night) ranging from a dramatic crimson, through to a lingering pink haze. Walking through the mallee in the gathering twilight, we could see the first evening stars glimmering on the horizon. We were still quite close to the Southern Ocean, although we could not see it.

'As far as I am concerned', I said to Ros, 'this is the last night of the trip. We have a long way to go, but it's all camp grounds and motels from here.'

Over dinner we drank a toast to the Williamses, the Leightons and other absent friends, and pledged to return to the west for the winter wildflower season as soon as we possibly could.

Shortly after midnight I left The Manor for a nocturnal pee. The crescent moon gave enough light not to need a torch, and the Southern Cross was blazing above with the kind of clarity you only get away from the cities and smog. I stood there for at least five minutes, savouring the ambience. It was also completely quiet, except for the occasional murmur of a passing car or truck from the Eyre Highway.

I felt a fierce exhilaration—not only for the beauty of the moment—but for being lucky enough to experience the privilege of enjoying wild and remote places that Australians must never take for granted.

Bibliography

Austin K A, *The Voyage of the Investigator 1801–1803: Commander Matthew Flinders, RN*, Rigby Ltd, Adelaide, 1964

Australian Explorers: A selection from their writings, Oxford University Press, London, 1958

Bowden R, *Women of the Land*, ABC Books, 1995

Cunningham C, *The Blue Mountains Rediscovered: beyond the myths of early Australian exploration*, Kangaroo Press, 1996

Dutton G, *In Search of Edward John Eyre*, The Macmillan Company of Australia, 1982

Faul J, *Life on the Edge: the far west coast of South Australia*, District Council of Murat Bay, Ceduna, 1988

Flinders M, *A Biographical Tribute to the Memory of Trim*, Angus & Robertson (an imprint of HarperCollins Publishers), Sydney, 1997

Hawdon J, *The Journal of a Journey from New South Wales to Adelaide: performed in 1938*, Georgian House, Melbourne, 1952

Hill E, *Water Into Gold*, Walkabout Pocketbooks, Ure Smith, 1969

James H C, *Western Australia: a pictorial parade of 150 years*, Rigby Ltd, Adelaide, 1979

Johnson L, *Albany: port with a past and a future*, Albany *Advertiser*, 1997

Stokes E, *The Desert Coast: Edward Eyre's expedition 1840–41*, Five Mile Press Pty Ltd, Victoria, 1993

Taylor J, *Australia's Southwest and Our Future*, Kangaroo Press, Sydney, 1990

Uren M & Stephens R, *Waterless Horizons*, Robertson & Mullens, Melbourne, 1945

Voices from a Vanishing Australia: recollections of the way things used to be, from ABC's *Word of Mouth*, ABC Enterprises, 1988